C000091913

The teacher of Ezra needs to understand the historical contou to draw hearers into its colourful world, and to see how this somewhat unfamiliar book points to Christ and finds fulfilment in Him. With his characteristic freshness, wit and insight, Adrian serves the Bible teacher admirably in both these tasks. I suspect that his guide will be an indispensable companion and aid for teachers of this rich book for many years to come.

Jonathan Griffiths
Lead Pastor, The Metropolitan Bible Church, Ottawa,
Canada

The Ezra part of the Nehemiah/ Ezra story is according to the Old Testament scholar Bruce Walkte 'A story the church needs to hear but rarely does'. We need to preach the text of Ezra again and learn the important lessons from that part of God's Word that the Spirit wants us to hear. I know of nothing more helpful in that task than Adrian's excellent book. It is more than a commentary – well researched and helpful as a commentary – but it makes all the right connections with a sound biblical theology and biblically shaped systematic theology to be really helpful to the preacher. With suggestions on how to preach the material in an expository fashion with sensible application it is gold dust for the preacher. In preaching Ezra it is an indispensable guide. Get it, read it, and above all preach this neglected part of Holy Scripture!

Wallace Benn
Retired Bishop, Diocese of Chichester, England
Author of forthcoming *Preaching the Word*, a commentary on
Ezra, Nehemiah & Esther

Before this book saw the world, I was privileged to listen to Adrian teaching on the book of Ezra at Cornhill. Adrian's clarity, passion and thorough treatment of the subject ignited many Cornhill students to study carefully, to put God's word into practice and then to teach it to others. Now Adrian's wisdom is available not only to Cornhill 'elite' but to everyone. The book that changed the course of its author's life won't leave you unmoved as Adrian unpacks its treasures. Highly recommended!

Taras Telkovsky
Pastor, Trinity Church, Minsk, Belarus

TEACHING
EZRA

From text to message

ADRIAN REYNOLDS

SERIES EDITORS: DAVID JACKMAN & JON GEMMELL

PT RESOURCES

CHRISTIAN
FOCUS

Copyright © Proclamation Trust Media 2018

ISBN: 978-1-78191-752-7

10 9 8 7 6 5 4 3 2 1

Published in 2018
by
Christian Focus Publications Ltd,
Geanies House, Fearn, Ross-shire,
IV20 1TW, Scotland, Great Britain.

with

Proclamation Trust Resources,
Willcox House, 140-148 Borough High Street,
London, SE1 1LB, England, Great Britain.
www.proctrust.org.uk

www.christianfocus.com

Cover design by Moose77.com

Printed and bound by
Bell & Bain, Glasgow.

Contents

With sincere and grateful thanks to God for
G. Eric Lane, my friend and mentor

❧ ❧ ❧

SERIES PREFACE

The aim of this series of books is very straightforward. It is to equip the expository preacher and Bible study leader to be able to preach and teach faithfully – warmly and appropriately applying the Scriptures to Christian life. As such, it is not a series of sermons nor is it a full-blown technical commentary. Rather, it focuses on helping the reader work out what the text says, means and how it may be applied. We do not want to take the hard work out of preparation, nor flatten preaching so that the resulting sermon could be preached in any place at any time. No, the preacher or teacher still needs to wrestle prayerfully with the text and so show himself or herself an unashamed and approved worker (2 Tim. 2:15). Our prayerful aim is that these books will be an aid and a guide rather than a replacement.

Our convictions about letting the text speak run deep. This is – at its heart – the expository method, where God says what God says rather than what we would rather have him say. We sometimes call this, 'giving God the microphone' or to use a different metaphor, 'putting God in the driving seat.' It is our belief that such preaching and teaching are the lifeblood of the local church. Each of these volumes seeks to serve those who labour in that invaluable ministry.

Teaching Ezra brings the number of published volumes to eighteen. Each is presented in a similar way. The Introductory Section contains basic 'navigation' material to get you into the text of Ezra, covering aspects like structure and planning a preaching series. This is also the place where any difficult issues that are particular to this Bible book are addressed. The main body of *Teaching Ezra* then works systematically through the text of Ezra, suggesting preaching or teaching units and also ideas for sermon outlines and questions for study groups.

This series matters to us because it is one of the most effective ways that we serve those in word ministry. We also do this through our conference programme and our online resources. But the book in your hand represents our focused work on one particular Bible book and – we trust and pray – that it will be helpful to you as you work hard, week in week out, to proclaim the unsearchable riches of Christ.

As always, we want to offer our thanks to those who have made this project a reality. Adrian's wife, Celia, checks all the Bible and book references, a long but important task. Jon Gemmell and Julia Marsden do the bulk of the detailed editing. As ever, our warm gratitude goes to the team at Christian Focus for their committed partnership in this project.

JONATHAN GEMMELL &
DAVID JACKMAN
Series Editors
London 2017

Author's Preface

Ezra is, for me, an intensely personal book. It is the book that God providentially used to bring me from the world of business into a life of ministry. I was sitting at home one Saturday afternoon a few years ago now and I decided to read a book of the Bible with which I was unfamiliar. I chose Ezra. But I never completed my task. I got stuck at Ezra 7:10, 'For Ezra had devoted himself to the study and observance of the Law of the Lord, and to teaching its decrees and laws in Israel.'

Study. Do. Teach. Ezra devoted himself to all three. It's an important triumvirate that today is taught in the very first week of the PT Cornhill Training Course in London where I served for a number of years. However, back then God used that single verse to begin to push me into full-time Christian ministry. There is more to the story than that of course! But that was the moment the process started and ever since, I have loved this book of the Bible.

I've had the privilege of preaching Ezra on a number of occasions. I preached Ezra to the members of Yateley

Baptist Church, where I first served. My preaching and ministry there was greatly helped by Eric Lane, to whom I owe a great debt, more than he realises I'm sure. I've since preached Ezra at East London Tabernacle, where I served as Honorary Associate Minister, and also to pastors in India – over an intense week's training. As those who have attended conferences with me will know, Ezra has also been a staple diet for workshops and talks, as well as being my pet subject on the Cornhill Course itself.

So, this Bible book is an old friend, precious personally, but also corporately, as I've seen the word of God working in the lives of others. I'm keen therefore that it is not neglected in favour of its 'big brother' Nehemiah. But many is the church which has a series on Nehemiah whilst overlooking Ezra. That's a shame because – as I hope to show – the books belong together and certainly deserve an equal hearing.

Ezra is a great book to teach others. The stories are exciting and fast paced. For sure, there are some difficult issues to address (not least in chapter 10), but the hard work is worthwhile. And, as is the case with many books from the last part of Old Testament history, Ezra has many and varied foreshadowings of the coming of Christ: it is, in other words, a wonderful book to preach Christologically.

My prayer is that this latest edition of the *Teaching...* series will enthuse and equip you so that Ezra and his message become as precious to you and your congregations as they are to me.

Adrian Reynolds
Market Harborough
February 2018

How to use this book

This book aims to help the preacher or teacher understand the central aim and purpose of the text in order to preach or teach it to others. Unlike a commentary therefore, it does not go into great exegetical detail. Instead it aims to help the teacher engage with the themes of Ezra, to keep the big picture in mind, and to think about how to present it to their hearers. I have deliberately written this book so that it can serve a number of different kinds of people; each will, I hope, get what they need from the volume:

- For those starting out in ministry and for whom expository preaching is a new idea, the book presents a 'start-to-finish' process of preparing a sermon, talk or study, including some suggested questions for a group.

- Those with more experience may find the sections which work through the text and suggest preaching/teaching units the most helpful parts of the book. These sections form the first half of

each chapter on the Bible text. The later sections
of those chapters suggest lines of application and
group study questions. These are intended to
supplement and affirm a teacher's own work rather
than replace it.

The chapters in Part One (the introductory section of the
book) should help every preacher and teacher.

'Part One: Introducing Ezra' examines the book's
themes and structure as well as some of the back story.
This material is crucial for our understanding of the
whole book, which in turn will shape the way we preach
each section to our congregations. I have included a short
section here on preaching the Old Testament as Christian
Scripture. Part One also suggests a division of Ezra's ten
chapters into thirteen preaching/teaching units – eight
units in Ezra 1–6 (The first return) and five units in
Ezra 7–10 (The second return).

Parts Two and Three then contain separate chapters
on each of these preaching units. The structure of each
of these chapters is the same: there is a brief introduction
to the unit followed by a section headed 'Listening to the
text.' This section outlines the structure and context of
the unit and takes the reader through a section-by-section
analysis of the text. All good Biblical preaching begins
with careful, detailed listening to the text and this is true
for Ezra as much as for any other book.

Each chapter then continues with a section called
'From text to message.' This suggests a main theme
and aim for each preaching unit (including how the unit
relates to the overall theme of the book) and then some
possible sermon outlines. Importantly, the aim section also

contains suggestions about how we preach Christ from this
Old Testament book.

All these suggestions are nothing more than that –
suggestions, designed to help the preacher think about
his own division of the text and structure of the sermon.
I am a great believer in every preacher constructing his
own outlines because these need to flow from our personal
encounter with God in the text. Downloading other
people's sermons or trying to breathe life into someone
else's outlines are strategies doomed to failure in my
experience. Doing this may produce a reasonable talk, but
in the long term it is disastrous to the preacher himself. If
a preacher is to speak from the heart of God to the hearts
of his congregation, he needs to live in the word and the
word needs to live in him.

However, these 'Text to message' sections will provide
the preacher or teacher with a number of starting points
for their own studies. They give a few very basic ideas about
how an outline on some of these passages might shape up.
There are also some bullet points suggesting possible lines
of application, with particular focus on how lines to Christ
may be drawn.

Each chapter on the Bible text concludes with some
suggested questions for a group Bible study. These questions
are grouped into two types: questions to help *understand*
the passage and questions to help *apply* the passage. Not
all the questions would be needed for an individual study
but they aim to give a variety of ideas for those who are
planning a study series.

The aim of good questions is always to drive the group
into the text to explore and understand its meaning more
fully. This keeps the focus on Scripture and reduces

speculation and the mere exchange of opinions. Remember, the key issues are always 'What does the text say?' and then 'What does it mean?' Avoid rushing quickly to the 'What does it mean to you?' type of question. Everyone needs to be clear on the original and intended meaning of a text before thinking about personal applications. Focusing on the intended meaning of a text will keep the Bible in the driving-seat of your study. It will stop the session being governed by the participants' opinions, prejudices or experiences!

These studies will be especially useful in those churches where Bible study groups are able to study a Bible book at the same time as it is preached, a practice I warmly commend. This allows small groups to drive home understanding and especially application in the week after the sermon has been preached. It ensures God's word is applied personally and specifically to the daily lives of the congregation.

Finally, many have found this series of books a useful aid in personal devotions, making use of the study questions to help understanding, application and prayer. Though they are not primarily designed for this purpose, we are delighted that they are used in such a way, for wherever God's word is faithfully proclaimed and taught, there God's voice is clearly heard.

INTRODUCING EZRA

1. Getting our bearings in Ezra

Introduction

The books of Ezra and Nehemiah tell of the last historical events recorded in the Old Testament. After these events there was a wait of around four hundred years before the coming of Jesus.

Ezra tells the story of how a group of Jews returned to Jerusalem after their exile to Babylon and set about rebuilding the temple. This building work began and got as far as constructing an altar and laying foundations before opposition from outsiders stopped the work for fifteen years. When the building work finally got going again, urged on by the prophets Haggai and Zechariah, the temple took a further four years to complete.

Around sixty years later, a priest/teacher of God's word called Ezra led another group of exiles back to Jerusalem from Babylon. His aim was to continue the restoration of temple worship and call God's people

to obey God's word. On his arrival in Jerusalem, Ezra
was devastated to find that God's people had disobeyed
God by intermarrying with pagans. The book ends with
Ezra's attempts to bring those who had disobeyed back
to repentance.

Ezra's companion book, Nehemiah, focuses on the
rebuilding of the walls of Jerusalem, a project which
follows the events recorded in Ezra.

Ezra is a relatively short book. Indeed, even a slow,
measured reading of the whole book takes less than
forty-five minutes.[1] It is not particularly complicated,
neither are its stories obscure. All of which makes it
perplexing that it is so little known, especially when
compared to its 'big brother' Nehemiah. As we shall
see, Ezra-Nehemiah are best thought of as one book,
but many is the church where a sermon or study series
will focus on the latter part to the exclusion of the
former.[2] Perhaps Nehemiah is a more acceptable hero
than Ezra, particularly in the light of Ezra's actions in
chapter 10. Nevertheless, it does seem to be something
of an evangelical oversight. And yet Ezra is a richly
rewarding book. The events it records come very near
the end of the covenant history of God's Old Testament
people, Israel. Jesus' first advent is coming soon. As we

---

1. NIV Audio Bible (London, UK: Hodder & Stoughton, 2014). This
means that the preacher or teacher can well afford the time to read
through the book several times to familiarise himself/herself with it, a
very worthwhile practice.

2. www.sermoncentral.com (a not necessarily reliable repository of
online audio) has 442 sermons on Nehemiah and only eighty-seven on
Ezra despite the books being comparable lengths. Accessed 9 December 2014.

read Ezra's ten short chapters, nearly all the themes that have been developing throughout the Old Testament are in view. There is a richness here which is condensed in a rare and a wonderful way. Time in this book is time that will pay great dividends.

Moreover, the themes of the book ring true and loudly today. In Ezra we see the sovereignty of God even in the lives and actions of pagan kings. We also see the people of God at their best. These are compelling stories with sharp contemporary applications.

If all this were not reason enough to preach and teach the book of Ezra, then we also need to remember that we too live in building times. True, we are not building a physical temple. But Christ has committed to building His church and Ezra gives us a glimpse into that great and eternal building project and what it is designed to achieve.

Structure

The macro-structure of the book of Ezra is reasonably straightforward to discern. This is because there is a large historical gap between the end of chapter 6 and the beginning of chapter 7 – some fifty something years (a period which chronologically includes the book of Esther). However, these two sections are more than just two halves of a book. Bob Fyall has shown how the two sections parallel one another closely in terms of the storyline.[3] I have repeated it here, together with some minor amendments:

---

3. See Fyall, R., *The message of Ezra & Haggai* (Nottingham, UK: IVP Books, 2010), p. 21, a structure that Fyall himself got from a colleague at his church, Dr Euan Dodds.

	Ezra Part 1 **Ezra 1–6** Commences in 538 B.C.	**Ezra Part 2** **Ezra 7–10** Commences in 458 B.C.
A king's edict under God's sovereign hand	Ezra 1:1-11	Ezra 7:1-28
A list of those returning	Ezra 2:1-70	Ezra 8:1-14
Sacrifices and work on their return	Ezra 3:1-13	Ezra 8:15-36
A problem or issue that needs resolving	Ezra 4:1-24 *In Part 1 the problem is external opposition.*	Ezra 9:1-5 *In Part 2 the problem is internal, disobedience to the Law.*
A resolution of the problem	Ezra 5:1–6:22	Ezra 9:6–10:44

Helpfully, Fyall points out that the problem in Part 1 is that pagans want to join Israel. In Part 2, the issue is reversed; Israel wants to join the pagans.

This structure serves the preacher or teacher well in two ways. First, it helps him make decisions about what we might call preaching units, that is, the appropriate length of passages to best serve a sermon or study series. Such units should reflect the aim or focus of the text.

As can be seen from the table prior, a series of ten such units does justice to the text (I will also suggest a slightly longer series than this, simply to accommodate the volume of material, particularly in Ezra 5–6 and 9–10).

Second, understanding the structure helps us see how the author's focus shifts between the two parts of the book. In Part 1 the focus is on the external pressures that the people of God face and how they deal with them. In Part 2 the focus shifts to the internal temptations to which they succumb. This definite shift needs to be reflected in the way Ezra is taught.

Overall, in broad terms the structure of Ezra is not complex and the serious student will be able to follow the flow of the passages within the book with relative ease.

Theme

As we read Ezra, the text continually reminds us of the sovereignty of God in the decision-making of kings, peoples and leaders. As we look at the structure of the book we see its twin sections: the first focusing on the restoration of temple worship and the second on honouring God by obedience to His word. So, as we study the text and structure of the book we can discern a dominant and unifying theme which runs throughout the book, what we sometimes call 'the melodic line' of the text. For Ezra I believe this to be:

The Lord providentially restores His people so that they can worship and honour Him.

Part 1 of the book is clearly about the temple rebuilding project. But all through the text we are encouraged to think in terms of what the temple is *for*, rather than simply what it *is*. It is the place where acceptable worship is offered to the Lord God, with sacrifices for sin and an acknowledgement of the Lord's goodness at its heart.

In Part 2 the focus shifts somewhat and the issue becomes one of Law-keeping. In particular, this focus is on the keeping of the law with regard to intermarriage. Ezra, the Law teacher, must unravel this mess when he returns to Jerusalem. Thus, this second half of the book is about obedience or, to put it better, honouring the Lord by keeping the Law.

In this way we can also see how Ezra's theme shapes our Christian understanding of the sovereign Lord's work amongst His people today. The work of the Spirit in the lives of believers through the proclaimed word of Christ is still being providentially used by God to make for Himself a people who will worship and honour Him. Ultimately that will not be in a temple made by human hands but in the city which has no need of a temple, for 'the Lord God Almighty and the Lamb are its temple' (Rev. 21:22).

Grasping this melodic line is essential for faithfully teaching the book of Ezra. If an individual message does not fit well within the framework of the whole book there is a real chance that we have not understood the passage in question properly. This is not an inviolable rule. Sometimes Bible writers do digress. However, on the whole it seems clear that Bible books are carefully and divinely crafted to make a certain point to a group of God's people; understanding this big theme and relating the individual passages to it is key to the task of expository preaching.

Context

Historical context

The historical context of Ezra is very important to understanding the book. Some Bible books can be understood fairly easily without knowing a great deal about the details of their historical context. Ezra, though, is an example of a book where knowing some of this background is a great help in getting to grips with the message the Holy Spirit is conveying.

This historical section is relatively long but I have summarised it at the end in a few bullet points for those who prefer a brief summary. All the history outlined here is internal to the Bible (it is not based on external sources) and so it represents the background that the Spirit has inspired for us.

The book of Ezra is a continuation of the story of the southern kingdom of Judah. This kingdom was formed after the death of Solomon when the original kingdom of the twelve tribes of Israel split in two. Broadly speaking, ten tribes formed what continued to be known as Israel (2 Chron. 10-12), with its capital in Samaria. The two southern tribes (Judah and Benjamin) were known as Judah from this point on (with a capital city of Jerusalem). This split happened in approximately 930 B.C.

The stories of the two kingdoms are contained in 1–2 Kings and 2 Chronicles (I have tried to use the Chronicles references where possible as this is the version of the story that most obviously continues on into Ezra). Though there were few godly kings, most continued the apostasy of the latter years of their predecessor, Solomon. Israel and Judah ceased to be the superpowers they had been in David and Solomon's time. The new kids on the block were Aram/ Syria[4] (also known by its capital city Damascus) and later Assyria. The history of Kings and Chronicles is often the story of alliances with these pagan nations, alliances

---

4. Old Testament nations should not, on the whole, be confused with their modern counterparts who share their names.

which are later broken and then resumed and enforced militarily. For the purposes of Ezra, we need to understand that things came to a head during the reign of Assyrian king Tilgath-Pileser who terrorised the northern kingdom (see 2 Chron. 28:20) and held the southern kingdom as a vassal state (2 Kings 16:7). Tilgath's son, Shalmaneser, brought the northern kingdom of Israel to an end when he discovered that her king, Hoshea, was secretly in league with Egypt (2 Kings 17:4). This final defeat of Israel took place in 722 b.c.

The resettlement policy of Assyria was to take everyone out of the land (2 Kings 17:6) and then to mix the Jews up with other nations and races and resettle them all over the Assyrian empire, with some returning to Israel itself (2 Kings 17:24). This gave rise to a mixed religion being practised in Israel. This mixed religion acknowledged Yahweh alongside a panoply of other gods so the author of 2 Kings can record, without a hint of contradiction, 'They worshipped the LORD, but they also served their own gods in accordance with the custom of the nations from which they had been brought. To this day they persist in their former practices. They neither worship the LORD nor adhere to the decrees and regulations, the laws and commands that the LORD gave the descendants of Jacob, whom he named Israel' (2 Kings 17:33-34).

In the southern kingdom, Judah, things were scarcely better. The Assyrian king, Sennacharib (Shalmaneser's successor but one), attacked Judah (2 Chron. 32:1), apparently because Judah's King, Hezekiah, had not paid the tribute that was due (2 Kings 18:14). Sennacharib's attack reached the walls of Jerusalem and ultimately ended in failure but not without effectively reducing Judah to little more than a city state. Following Judah's victory (and the beginning of a decline in Assyrian fortunes), Hezekiah foolishly welcomed envoys from the latest powerhouse, Babylon (2 Kings 20:12).

Hezekiah's immediate successors in Judah also stirred the anger of the Lord and Josiah's brief godly reign was not enough to assuage this. The writing was on the wall: 'Nevertheless, the LORD did not turn away from the heat of his fierce anger which burned against Judah because of all that Manasseh had done to arouse his anger. So the LORD said, "I will remove Judah also from my presence as I removed Israel, and I will reject Jerusalem, the city I chose, and this temple, about which I said, My Name shall be there".' (2 Kings 23:26-27).

Things came to a head in Judah during the reign of Jehoahaz who was defeated by an attack from Egypt (2 Chron. 36:3). The Egyptian king made Jehoahaz's brother, Jehoiakim, king in his place but this new king of Judah was attacked and defeated by Nebuchadnezzar of Babylon in 606 B.C. This is when the temple was first looted. It is probably the moment too when Daniel and his friends were carried off to Babylon (Daniel 1:1-6). Jehoiakim's son, Jehoiachin, replaced him as ruler in Judah but he was quickly summoned to Babylon together with the remaining treasures (2 Chron. 36:9-10). Nebuchadnezzar installed Zedekiah, another member of Judah's royal family, as the new puppet king over those still living in the land. Zedekiah lasted for eleven years in Judah but in the end was attacked by Babylon. The temple was then finally destroyed and all the remaining treasures stolen (2 Chron. 36:18-19). Importantly, the settlement policy of Nebuchadnezzar was markedly different from the policy of his Assyrian counterparts. Far from the land being resettled, Judah was left in ruins and all the exiles were carried off in 586 B.C. to Babylon (2 Chron. 36:20). The land was left desolate and empty.

In exile the people were ministered to by the prophets Jeremiah and Ezekiel, though they did not always appreciate their messages! It was clear that the exile had happened because of the nation's rebellion against the Lord. The exile was the ultimate covenant curse (see Deut. 28:49-52). However, the exiles were told to prosper in Babylon (Jer. 29). Though there was a sadness about being away from Jerusalem and being under the wrath of God (Ps. 137), we are not to think that they spent seventy years with bags packed, ready to go at a moment's notice. To do so would minimise the significance of Ezra 1.

The book of 2 Chronicles ends with the same verses with which Ezra begins (36:22-23 is repeated in Ezra 1:1-2). In other words, we readers are meant to see the covenant story continuing through the exile and on into the people's return. This great moment was heralded by the defeat of the Babylonian empire and the rise of a new power, Persia, a conquest that took place in 539 B.C.

In summary:

- 930 B.C.: David's kingdom splits in two, following the death of his son, Solomon.

- 722 B.C.: The northern kingdom (Israel) is defeated by Shalmaneser of Assyria.

- 606 B.C.: The southern kingdom (Judah) is first attacked by Nebuchadnezzar of Babylon; Daniel is carried off to Babylon.

- 586 B.C.: The final defeat and destruction of
  Jerusalem by Nebuchadnezzar; a remnant is taken
  into exile in Babylon.

- 539 B.C.: Cyrus of Persia conquers the Babylonian
  kingdom and allows Jewish exiles to return.

Theological context

It is important however to see the context of Ezra as more than
just a series of dates and kings, like some kind of old-fashioned
history lesson. This historical detail with all its accuracy is
helpful in reinforcing the historicity of the Ezra story. The
Bible is never just history though, rather it is history with a
purpose. It is a theological story set in an historical framework.

It is helpful to understand how the story of Ezra relates
to the three key covenants of the Old Testament.

First, we have the Abrahamic covenant of Genesis 12.
There, God promises His servant Abraham that He will
richly bless him, giving him land and making his descendants
both numerous and also a blessing to the world. We know
from our Biblical theology (how the whole Bible fits together)
that these promises are fulfilled in Christ (see Gal. 3:16) and
to those who are in Christ (see Rom. 4:16, which cites the
same Genesis reference). Throughout the Old Testament we
see physical shadows of these deeper realities which are found
in Jesus. It is unsurprising therefore that we see the same
echoes in the book of Ezra, with perhaps particular emphasis
on the continuation of the nation made up of Abraham's
descendants, even if in Ezra's day it is vastly reduced in size.

After the Exodus from slavery in Egypt, God gives His
people the Law, the covenant with Moses. This Law is closely
and intimately linked with God's people's life in the land
(see for example, Deut. 4:1). It is true that Christians cannot

always agree on the precise nature of the relationship between the Abrahamic and Mosaic covenants. Nevertheless, for our purposes we can see that this Mosaic Law-covenant is still in operation in Ezra's time, governing the comings and goings of the people of God. This is made very clear in passages such as Ezra 3:1-6 and 7:13-26. We know that with the coming of Christ the Law ceased to function in the same way, that is, as a unified code which cannot be broken up. It finds its fulfilment in Christ and so, whatever our particular view of the Law, we should not expect it to operate for believers in the way that it does in the book of Ezra.

Thirdly, there is the Davidic covenant. After the conquest of the land the people demanded a king, in effect rejecting the rule of God over them. God graciously grants their request and from this inauspicious beginning comes one of the most exalted promises of the Old Testament as God promises David, 'Your house and your kingdom shall endure forever before me; your throne shall be established forever' (2 Sam. 7:16). Ironically, this is the covenant that looks most 'at risk' in Ezra. The last kings of Judah (Jehoiakim, Jehoiachin and Zedekiah) are a pretty sorry lot. There seems to be little hope for a continuation of a godly Davidic line through men such as these and the exile only seems to confirm this dilemma. Ezra never directly addresses this point – there is no overt mention of 2 Samuel 7 nor of David nor of the promises made at other times about a restored Davidic kingdom. Nevertheless, there is a hint in Ezra that this Davidic covenant is continuing, for Zerubbabel is a governor of Judah and so a kind of quasi-king. When we read the genealogy of Jesus in Matthew 1 this hint is reinforced as we find that Zerubbabel was a descendant of David. Moreover, the preaching of Zechariah is a key element of the story of Ezra and the continuation of the Davidic promise is central to Zechariah's message. We read the details of Zechariah's message in the book which bears his name.

In other words, we need to understand that the people of Ezra lived in the shadow of these three great covenants. However, for the most part the story of Ezra is largely concerned with the Abrahamic and Mosaic covenants rather than the Davidic promises, although these should not be ignored.

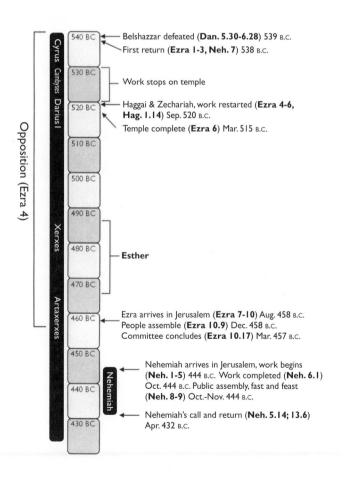

Timeline for Ezra-Nehemiah

Notes on the timeline

- Ascertaining the reigns of kings in ancient history is not an exact science. Dates are often different in various commentaries by one or two years as there is not always universal agreement over whether the first year of a reign is counted as inclusive or not. However, for our purposes the dates of reigns given above are sufficiently close to allow us to see how the book works chronologically.

- The chronology clearly supports the division outlined above with the book having two distinct halves.

- Preachers should note the interaction and continuity with books such as Daniel, Haggai, Zechariah, Esther and Nehemiah.

- One Persian king is not mentioned in Ezra – that is Cambyses, Cyrus' son. More precisely he is known as Cambyses II (his grandfather, Cyrus' father, had the same name). His omission is puzzling although it may be that his reign was simply seen as a continuation of his father's. Darius (Cambyses' successor) was not from the same family but was Cambyses' personal bodyguard.

- Xerxes (Esther's husband) is referred to as Ahasuerus in the ESV and some other translations.

- Chapter 4 of Ezra includes incidents from the reigns of several kings, some from later times, but the chapter is represented in the text as explaining the main Ezra story during the latter years of Cyrus' reign and early years of King Darius. There is more discussion on the point in Part 2 of this book.

- In general, dates of this period are stated very precisely which allows us to be specific about, for example, the length of the journey from Babylon to Jerusalem. Not only does this precision give a note of authenticity, it also resonates with a modern way of reading history which is characteristically very precise. However, despite this precision, preachers need to be careful to avoid thinking that Ezra-Nehemiah is written as modern history in the way we would usually consider this.

- Malachi is clearly post-exilic. It is, though, never specifically time-referenced in the rest of the Bible and so is difficult to put into this timeline. Clearly the temple is in operation (Mal. 1:8-10) and the most obvious dating would put it around the time of Ezra Part 2 and Nehemiah.

Authorship

There are a number of possibilities when it comes to determining the author of the book. Traditionally, Ezra himself has often been identified as the author of the 1&2 Chronicles series as well as Ezra-Nehemiah. This theory is largely based on the apocryphal books that also bear the latinized form of his name, Esdras. There, Ezra is represented as almost solely responsible for the restoration of the Scriptures following their loss during the exile. The books of the Bible are said to have been dictated to Ezra's team of scribes verbatim by the 'Most High' (2 Esdras 14:37-48). This extraordinary story in the Apocrypha is riddled with difficulty for those with a high view of Scripture and revealed Canon. Not only is the number of Old Testament books wrong (ninety-four), some books are said to be retained for only the worthy to read. Moreover, the idea of dictation replacing inspiration is problematic.[5] If this is our only source for determining Ezra as the principal author of the book that bears his name, then it should be quickly rejected.

A second possibility is that the two books of Ezra and Nehemiah are autobiographical and Ezra is responsible for his part and Nehemiah for his. Some parts of Nehemiah are certainly written in the first person singular. However, the timeline hints against this and there is internal evidence to suggest that this is unlikely to be the case (Neh. 12:10-11 goes well beyond Nehemiah's probable death). We could say the same for Ezra itself. Some parts are clearly autobiographical; however, other parts predate the priest.

It is most likely that the author is the Chronicler. We can say with certainty that the beginning of Ezra picks up where 2 Chronicles leaves off. There is also some overlap between the two books. This is helpful to us because we need to keep seeing the continuity that Scripture presents; in Ezra we see the covenant people of God living still under the Mosaic Law Covenant and looking forward to the coming of the long-promised Messiah. At their best the

---

5. Although, interestingly, it is possible to speculate that Muhammad 'learnt' some of his ideas for divine inscripturation from this Apocryphal story.

people of Ezra's day are no better off than King David or Josiah. The promised heart-change, called for so often in the prophets, is still needed and still awaited.

Relationship to Nehemiah

In the Jewish Scriptures Ezra-Nehemiah is one scroll. The first record we have of its division into two books is in the writings of Origen (3rd Century). There are clear connections between the two books:

- One chapter is repeated verbatim (Ezra 2 and Neh. 7).

- Many of the characters appear in both books (in particular, Ezra features in Nehemiah).

- The same kings dominate the landscape (in particular, Artaxerxes, Ezra's king and Nehemiah's boss).

- The same themes recur, especially in terms of opposition and God's sovereignty over the rebuilding projects (first, the temple, then the walls).

Ideally, the preacher or teacher should fight to keep Ezra and Nehemiah together, if for no other reason than it avoids repeating all the background work. However, a stand-alone series on Ezra is clearly possible and even desirable if a church has had a semi-regular diet of Nehemiah on its own.

2. Why should we preach and teach Ezra?

We have already begun to see some of the key reasons why a sermon or study series on Ezra would bear fruit. Of course, first and foremost it is part of divine Scripture and on this basis alone, Ezra warrants our attention. But more broadly, the resonant themes of the sovereignty of God working through human action to make a people for Himself are relevant in any age, culture or setting. Most importantly perhaps, there are rich themes anticipating the coming of Christ. These themes warrant further introduction.

Preaching Christ from the Old Testament (and Ezra in particular)

One of the hardest tasks for a Christian preacher is to preach Christ from these Old Testament stories. As we have seen, the theological context is not just the covenant made with Abraham but also the narrower context of the Mosaic covenant (closely linked as it is with living in the promised land) and the Davidic covenant too (connected to kingship). Both of these latter covenants find their fulfilment in Christ Jesus Himself who is both the ultimate law-keeper and the long-promised Messiah, descendent of David. It is a mistake to think that we live directly under those covenants today in every detail now when they stand fulfilled in Christ. We are Christians living under the New Covenant. Unfortunately, though, it is quite possible (and relatively common) for these Old Testament stories to be preached as though the coming of Christ had made little, if any, difference.

This mistake will be most obvious if we always simplistically equate the people of God *then* with the people of God *now*. Tempting as this may be, it will often lead us down some unhelpful paths. We must not say that, because it *sometimes* gives the 'right' application that it will *always* do so. There is never a substitute for the hard work of looking closely at the text, thinking about it Christologically and then drawing appropriate lines of application.[6]

For example, cutting these corners in Ezra 10 is almost certain to lead to some wrong applications. If the preacher or teacher has not done the hard work of thinking about the passage as a New Covenant message then it would be perfectly possible to say to a congregation, 'All those married to unbelievers must divorce them now!' Hopefully, we can all see that this *cannot* be an appropriate application, for God hates divorce and divorce is only ever a permission rather than a command. However, we sometimes use similar reasoning to get to other applications from books like Ezra which sound much more acceptable and 'Christian'. We need to be careful to adopt a consistent approach to ensure we get to the right answer every time.

Our contention is that the only way to do this is for us to think about preaching Christ from these passages. Two obvious questions present themselves: *Can* we preach Christ from an Old Testament text in Ezra, and if so,

---

6. There is a lot more on this process in Helm, D., *Expositional Preaching* (Wheaton, USA: Crossway Books, 2014). His excellent summaries are themselves based on instructions from R. C. Lucas, who helped found The Proclamation Trust.

must we? [7] The answer to the first question is a clear and resounding 'Yes'. Jesus said of our Old Testament books, 'These are the very Scriptures that testify about me' (John 5:39). The answer to the second question is more contentious. I believe that the answer to this too is found in Jesus' words, for He continued, 'Yet you refuse to come to me to have life.' Life in all its fullness is found in Christ and in Him alone. As preachers of the New Covenant, our task is to preach Christ; this is precisely the work that Paul, for example, took on in Corinth (see 1 Cor. 1:23, 2:2). To put it another way, the preacher of Ezra or the Bible study leader has no authority to do anything *but* lead people to Christ from these inspired texts. It is in carefully doing this that we shall find ourselves making the right applications.

Moreover, in Ezra there is a richness for the New Covenant teacher that is not always found in other Old Testament books. Christ is revealed progressively in the Old Testament. The promise of Genesis 3:15 develops into the promises made to Abraham (Gen. 12). The Law anticipates the coming of a prophet and in its Levitical offerings it shows us the need for atonement. By the time of 1 & 2 Kings the Davidic covenant is front and centre. Yet all of these threads develop and deepen as the coming of the long-promised Messiah nears. By the time of Ezra, therefore, we see a wonderful breadth of Christological application. The challenge for the preacher is not always, 'how do I preach Christ from this text?' but rather, 'what do I limit myself to?'

---

7. These are the two questions that Dale Ralph Davis asks in a short section of *The word became fresh* (Fearn, UK: Christian Focus, 2006), p. 134-138. His answers are 'Yes' and 'No'. I respectfully disagree.

However, there are two extremes to avoid here. One extreme reduces Old Testament preaching down to a single message, something along the lines of 'look how God is fulfilling His promises.' Such preaching and teaching ignore the detail and colour of the text as well as its particular focus. The other extreme sees Christ popping out – as it were – at every moment from behind every bush and rock. The Old Testament does not function in this way; it is not a kind of Christian version of 'Where's Wally?'[8]

Nevertheless, there are echoes, shadows and copies of what is to come in Christ Jesus and the preacher or teacher needs to be aware of these. Here are just a few lines of thought:

1. In the **faithfulness of God**, we see the covenant-keeping of the Lord. The book is introduced with a deliberate reminder that God is keeping His promises. Whilst the Old Testament message is bigger and deeper than the (sometimes minimalist) maxim: 'God is keeping His promises', we need to understand that it is not less than that. The openings of the Gospels (particularly Matthew and Luke) make it clear that the Scriptures are being fulfilled.

2. In the **sovereignty of God**, we see the covenant promises of God being worked out, sometimes against all the odds. The Lord even uses pagan kings and their rules to bring about His purposes. It is in precisely along these lines that Peter speaks at Pentecost about the death of Christ (see Acts 2:23).

---

8. A children's series where readers are invited to find one character in a very detailed picture. It's known as *Where's Waldo?* in the USA.

3. **Zerubbabel** is the key leader of the people. He is not a
   king but he is in the kingly line, (a point made forcibly
   in Matt. 1:12-13). The covenant promise to David has
   not failed: his line has not died out.

4. The leadership of Israel in the first part of Ezra is often
   presented as the team of Zerubbabel and **Joshua the
   High Priest.** Joshua receives almost equal focus in
   the book. His name is mentioned at key moments,
   particularly with relation to the temple rebuilding and
   sacrificial worship (see below). The priestly line always
   takes us to the Great High Priest (Heb. 5-7).

5. The story of the book of Ezra takes place entirely in
   the context of **Law and sacrifice.** Indeed, Law keeping
   and sacrifice are key elements in passages such as 3:1-6
   and the king's instruction to Ezra in 7:11-28. We can
   see Christological fulfilment both in broad terms and
   in the detail. In broad terms, Jesus fulfils the Law (see
   Matt. 5:17). The Law had a place in Israel's national
   life 'until Christ came' (Gal. 3:24). This is also true in
   the specifics: particular elements of the Law are brought
   into the foreground in Ezra. Chapter 3 focuses on the
   burnt offerings and the Feast of Tabernacles, 6:19-22
   describes the first Passover in the new Temple and Ezra's
   prayer in 9:6-15 makes much of the Law's commands
   against intermarriage.

6. It is impossible to read Ezra without appreciating the
   central theme of **temple** rebuilding. The first part of
   the book majors on this project, with all its ups and
   downs. Whilst Part 2 of Ezra takes place some decades
   later, the temple is still a key theme (see 7:17 and 10:1,

for example), even though there has been a major shift
of focus here towards Law observance. This theme of
temple building is picked up in the New Testament
(for example, 1 Pet. 2:4-10) and provides a rich seam of
nuanced applications.

7. The **prophetic voice of God** in Haggai and Zechariah
takes a key place in the story at 5:1-2, reinforced at 6:14.
It is made clear that the temple's completion was due,
at least in part, to their prophetic intervention. In the
book of Zechariah, we read of God's promise of future
deliverance. It seems that it is this promise which
reignites the present work on the temple. For example,
Zechariah records God's promise of the coming of a king
on a donkey (Zech. 9:9-13), a promise which prefigures
the Triumphal Entry. We have the word of the prophets
'as something completely reliable' (2 Pet. 1:19).

8. Finally, we cannot ignore that in the early chapters of
Ezra we see the **people of God** at their best. It is tempting
to draw direct lines of application but we must be very
cautious in doing so without any New Testament control.
As we have already seen, this can lead us down some wrong
paths. Better I think to see the people of God at their best
as showing us Christ. He is the true Israelite who was
called out of Egypt (Hosea 11:1 quoted in Matt. 2:15).
Insomuch as there are lessons for us to learn, we must see
them as those who are in Christ, the true Israelite. This
may seem like a 'long way round' in terms of application
but it will always help us avoid false lines.[9]

---

9. This is not the place to develop this theme further, but it is clearly
explained in Helm.

Challenges in preaching Ezra

Ezra is a relatively short and straightforward book without many of the internal complexities and theological challenges that present themselves in some books. Nevertheless, it is worth being aware of three particular issues that do arise.

Detailed lists

First, lists of names and numbers seem very unappealing to congregations. These form a substantial part of the book (1:9-10; 2:1-70; 8:1-14; 10:18-43). It is tempting to skip over these or – at best – preach and teach them as a kind of addendum to other narrative passages. However, we need to be reminded that these words too are part of inspired Scripture and some work on them will yield valuable insights, for the lists are always more than just lists.

For example, the short list in chapter 1 indicates the way that God has preserved the articles stolen from the Jerusalem temple and identified in 2 Chronicles. That they were counted out shows a precision and also an interest in their return. As we shall see, the list in chapter 2 is full of interesting and useful detail. The final list in chapter 10 gives, if nothing else, an estimate of the size of the problem of intermarriage and records the names of those found guilty.

We need to remember that genealogy and lineage is a key element of Israelite identity. We are beginning to reclaim some of this today in the West with our obsession with family history. But to many these lists still seem irrelevant and obscure. We owe it to our congregations to bring them alive, not least to present a robust doctrine of the word of God. For skipping these apparently hard parts sends all kinds of messages about a lack of confidence in inspiration.

Long narrative passages

In order to do justice to a number of the stories in Ezra there are some parts of the book that are best taken together. For example, 5:1-6:12 is a reasonably long unit with lots of detail. It would be possible to strip out 5:1-2 and preach just on the prophesying of Haggai and Zechariah (indeed, I have done so). However, I would contend that doing so is not really doing justice to that particular text which is controlled by 6:13-15 (see chapter below).

It is not possible however to retain the pace and continuity of the story and also to make something of every small detail. A balance needs to be struck. The detail in Old Testament narrative is generally there to give colour and pace to a story rather than make a theological point at every turn. Too *slow* an approach can negate the form of the text. Scripture is inspired in both form *and* content.

Chapters 5 and 6 are perhaps a case in point. The exchange of letters in these chapters is full of detail. The author is drawing a clear distinction between these and the previous exchanges (4:9-22) and showing how the original decree is found and acted upon. But it is not, for example, a theological treatise on how secular governments can and should fund Christian work (6:8).

One other point is worth making. For the most part, reading long passages takes much less time than people think and this should not be a reason for, in effect, abbreviating Scripture.

The last difficult chapter

Thirdly, some preachers and teachers are put off by the apparent brutality of chapter 10. Unlike some other difficult passages in the Old Testament, the issue here is not one of physical violence. Rather, what we see in this chapter appears to be a misogynistic over-reaction to a real problem – that of intermarriage. Moreover, 21st Century teachers worry, not just that the passage sounds harsh to modern ears, but that the obvious application ('divorce your non-Christian spouse') cannot be right.

Indeed. And – as we shall see – a proper assessment of the passage does not lead us to that conclusion. Nevertheless, there is no avoiding the fact that this chapter is a difficult passage to preach and teach, especially as hearers will inevitably draw conclusions about it as soon as they hear it read.

But nowhere else in the Bible do we avoid difficult passages and we should not do so here. In fact, ideas and concepts that we find challenging often lie at the root of key Christian doctrines – not least the pouring out of the settled wrath of God the Father upon His Son as a means of securing our redemption.

An introductory sermon or Bible study

Elsewhere, I have suggested that an introductory sermon or Bible study can be a good way to start a series in an unfamiliar book.[10] That is particularly the case where there is a controlling passage in the New Testament which helps make sense of the Old Testament Scripture. I don't believe there is any such dominant New Testament control for Ezra nor is there a necessity for such help before launching a series for this particular book.

---

10. See Reynolds, A., *Teaching Numbers* (Fearn, UK: Christian Focus & PT Resources, 2013), p. 43.

However, it is useful for a congregation to hear and grasp at least some of the historical and theological background. Quite how a Bible teacher delivers this is a matter of personal preference and congregational accommodation. I have often taken a few minutes before a series begins to give some background.

One sermon from 2 Chronicles might lend itself to fulfilling this task and provide helpful background material. This is not as haphazard as it sounds because of the clear continuity that is established in 2 Chronicles 36:22-23 and the first few verses of Ezra. Such an introduction would not be necessary for congregations who are well versed in Bible history and therefore, who understand terms like 'Exile' immediately. For others though it might well be helpful.

Second Chronicles chapter 36 makes clear some important contextual points for understanding Ezra:

- The Exile was deserved and part of God's judgment against Judah. The constant refrain of the passage is that the kings do evil in God's sight (vv. 5, 8, 9, 12, 13, 14).

- God was patient with Judah and tried to arrest her decline (vv. 15-16). However, His prophets were 'mocked' and 'despised.' Rejecting the word of the Lord eventually ended with the nation being rejected by the Lord.

- The Exile was not the end of the story (v. 21). In fact the author is able to speak almost poetically about desolation in Jerusalem ('enjoyed its sabbath rests'). The Lord still speaks His word. It may have

been rejected but His sure and certain promises
continue and there is light at the end of the tunnel
– a bright light.

And so begins Ezra.

3. Ideas for a preaching or teaching series in Ezra

Ezra is not a particularly long book (ten chapters). It divides easily up to make a relatively short preaching or teaching series. However, there are one or two key questions for the preacher or teacher to grapple with. First, decisions have to be made about whether and how to include Nehemiah in the series. As we have seen, Ezra-Nehemiah sits comfortably as one book with similar themes and characters. In fact Ezra Part 2 sits more naturally with Nehemiah than it does with Ezra Part 1, certainly in historical terms. It might therefore seem obvious to tackle both books together.

This is not necessarily the right approach, however. Joining both books together makes for a considerably longer series and the preacher needs to ensure he does justice to both books rather than doing a kind of hatchet job on the text. For example, it is surely better to tackle Ezra steadily than just to cherry-pick three or four 'purple passages'. Moreover, the book of Nehemiah may be considerably more familiar to congregations. Preaching Ezra may therefore be a kind of 'last piece of the puzzle' that a congregation needs.

Second, decisions need to be made about the speed of a series. As this volume suggests, there are some chapters that can be naturally grouped together – chapters 1 and 2, and chapters 5 and 6, are obvious examples. Though these groupings make long passages to read, the stories in them flow naturally.

A thirteen part series

This book divides the ten chapters of Ezra into thirteen teaching sections. No doubt there is room to go even more slowly (for example, taking 1:1 as an introductory sermon). Nevertheless, I contend that the approach I suggest here reflects the pace of the book appropriately whilst not missing the detail it contains.

1. The LORD in control   Ezra 1: 1-11
2. The people at their best   Ezra 2:1-70
3. First things first   Ezra 3:1-6
4. Joy and sadness   Ezra 3:7-13
5. Surrounded by enemies   Ezra 4:1-5
6. Opposition works…   Ezra 4:6-24
7. …oh, no it doesn't!   Ezra 5:1–6:12
8. Finishing with a feast   Ezra 6:13-22
9. Introducing Ezra   Ezra 7:1-10
10. Another king, another letter Ezra 7:11-28
11. Home again   Ezra 8:1-36
12. Disobedience and confession   Ezra 9:1-15
13. Putting things right   Ezra 10: 1-44

A six part series

A briefer series that would still do justice to the text might be achieved over six weeks. Ironically, shorter series are often harder to deliver as the preacher or teacher has to work very hard at communicating quite complex stories *and* find time to apply them Christologically. I find preaching this way harder rather than easier. Nevertheless, the following series could still do justice to the focus of the different passages:

1.	The LORD in control	Ezra 1–2
2.	Worship starts	Ezra 3
3.	Worship stops	Ezra 4
4.	Worship restored	Ezra 5–6
5.	A new teacher	Ezra 7–8
6.	A renewed covenant	Ezra 9–10

The lessons and applications in this shorter series would necessarily need to be broader.

Haggai and Zechariah

The preaching of Haggai and Zechariah is clearly central to the plot in chapters 5 and 6 of Ezra. It is their preaching which restarts the work and is identified as a key factor in the completion of the temple (6:14). It is therefore tempting to include some or all of their prophecies (which are recorded in the books which bear their names) in a series on Ezra. One might go so far as to break a series in Ezra at 5:1 and preach right through these prophetic books. That would surely be a mistake. The inspired author has given us a connection to these prophets but he has not seen fit to make a very close link to their actual words – none of which are quoted in Ezra. We should be similarly reticent. Occasional quotes might serve us well and add light to the sermon or study. Quoting or looking up long passages is unlikely to serve the purpose of Ezra. We will end up preaching the prophetic books, which are complex themselves (especially Zechariah), and losing the focus of the text of Ezra.

That is not to say there is no connection between Ezra and the books of Haggai and Zechariah. Ezra gives us the historical context of both these prophetic books and knowing that context is a great help in preaching their messages. The hermeneutical key to both Haggai and Zechariah is to ask, 'What is it about this particular prophecy that got the people building again?' Why, for example, does the amazing word spoken about Joshua in Zechariah 3 rekindle the building flame? The divinely inspired connection between Ezra and these prophetic books prompts us to ask such questions and helps us understand them correctly.

THE FIRST RETURN (EZRA 1–6) (538 B.C.–516 B.C.)

1. The LORD in control (Ezra 1:1-11)

King Cyrus of Persia is moved by God to command the exiled Jews to return to Jerusalem and rebuild the temple. The Jews are moved by God to go back. Cyrus gives them back the items that were stolen from the temple when Jerusalem was conquered.

Introduction

The very first section of Ezra sets the tone and context for the whole book. Not only does this first chapter set the historical context (the early reign of King Cyrus of Persia), it also sets a definite theological note: this is the Sovereign Lord at work, fulfilling His promises and overseeing even the heart of a pagan king. In the book of Ezra we watch men and women thinking, choosing and making their own decisions (and living with the consequences) but we are never left to think that God's sovereignty is either ineffective or intermittent. It is a question of both/and rather than either/or.

In this first chapter we are also introduced to some other key features which will recur again and again:

- Official edicts. These will also feature heavily in Ezra 4, 5, 6 and 7;

- Tabular lists. Here we have a list of things (the temple inventory) but the same kind of list form is repeated in Ezra 2, 8 and 10 with lists of people;

- Identification of key names. These are sometimes perplexing (see discussion of Sheshbazzar below) but these names were clearly known to the first readers.

In approaching chapter 1 the preacher or teacher faces a dual temptation. On the one hand, it is possible to make *too much* of some of the details of the passage: for example, the exact nature of Cyrus' faith in God (or otherwise) in 1:2, or the exact use of the particular temple dishes in the inventory of 1:9. These words and phrases are not explained in the text, so in making much of them we will only be speculating. These details bring colour to the narrative to bring the text alive rather than defining the author's key idea.

On the other hand, there is also the temptation to over-look remarkably significant phrases such as 1:1 and 1:5 (which we will explore further below) or the echoes of the Exodus that are found in the way that neighbours assist the returning exiles.

As with a new series on any Bible book it is important to set Ezra in its immediate context. As we have already seen there is a direct and obvious continuity with the covenant story so far. This is shown by the fact that the first few verses of Ezra are a direct repeat of the last few verses of 2 Chronicles. Clearly we are intended to see Ezra's account (together with the related accounts of Nehemiah and Esther) as the next part of the story of God's covenant people. As we read on we discover that we are actually reading the last chapter of the history of God's people before the coming of their long-promised Messiah.

Listening to the text

Context and structure

The first chapter of Ezra introduces us to the three main characters in our story: The Lord God Yahweh, the pagan rulers of Persia (King Cyrus and his successors) and the people of God.

The way the three characters are introduced is significant. We are introduced to Cyrus in the context of God's sovereign rule (v. 1) and we are introduced to the people of God in precisely the same way (v. 5). We are to see right from the start that there is really only one major character, God Himself; the book we are beginning is an account of the outworking of His sovereign rule and promises in the world and His people.

This truth will help us when we come to preach or teach Chapter 1. It shows us that our focus should be less on Cyrus and the people of God and their various decisions and more on the sovereign and faithful God who moved their hearts to take the actions we read about here.

Having made this overarching truth clear, we now turn to the structure of the chapter. The text divides naturally into two, with the first part dealing with Cyrus, the pagan king and the second with the exiled people of God:

- God and His king (1:1-4)

- God and His people (1:5-11)

These two sections are identified by the key repeated phrase 'moved the heart' (v. 1 and v. 5) ('stirred the spirit' – ESV). We are told that God moved the hearts of both the pagan king and the faithful exiles. God's action lies behind all these human decisions. Ezra is giving us a theological commentary on these historical events. Again and again as we read on we will be shown that God is at work in and through human actions to fulfil His purposes.

Ezra chapter 2 is a list of the particular people whose hearts God moved to go to Jerusalem. The content of these first two chapters of Ezra are clearly very closely related and you may choose to preach these two chapters together in a single sermon. In the next chapter of this book I will suggest how you might approach doing this. However, there is enough detail and focus in each chapter to teach them separately and this will be the primary approach of this *Teaching…* volume.

Working through the text
God and His king (1:1-4)

God behind it all
Right at the start we are given a date marker for the first section of the book. The events described here take place in the first year of the Persian King Cyrus who assumed the throne in 538 B.C. after overthrowing the Babylonian empire. These events are also described in Daniel 5-6.

Confusingly, in the book of Daniel, the first king of Persia is called Darius (see Dan. 5:31) and Cyrus appears to be listed as ruling after him (Dan. 6:28). In Ezra this order appears to be reversed as Ezra 4:5 reads, 'They bribed officials…during the entire reign of Cyrus king of Persia down to the reign of Darius king of Persia.' It seems that the order apparent in Ezra 4:5 is correct and that Cyrus was the first king of Persia with King Darius following him. Certainly other historical evidence supports this view. The references in Daniel probably indicate that Cyrus took the name Darius as a 'throne name', that is, his formal title as monarch, as opposed to the name he used day to day. We are familiar with this idea in much more recent history. For example, King Edward VIII was known as David and King George VI was known as Bertie. If Darius was Cyrus' throne name, as seems likely, Daniel 6:28 should be read as, 'So Daniel prospered during the reign of Darius, that is, the reign of Cyrus' (NIV, margin). This reading is grammatically possible and provides the most likely solution to this apparent contradiction.

Coming back to Ezra 1, what is crystal clear is that King Cyrus is God's king. God is behind this pagan king's action as verse 1 makes explicit. Other Bible books, especially Isaiah, also speak of Cyrus as God's king, a ruler whom God has chosen to do His will. For example, in Isaiah God speaks of Cyrus as 'my shepherd' (Isa. 44:28) and as 'my anointed' (Isa. 45:1).

Ezra 1:1 highlights that God moves Cyrus' heart 'in order to fulfil the word of the Lord spoken by Jeremiah.' In other words, this is not just God's sovereignty on display but His covenant faithfulness too. God uses His sovereign power to keep His word to His people. This is an important truth. God's rule is not capricious or random – He always acts in sovereign power in accordance with His nature, character and promises. And so it is here.

It is not immediately obvious which word of the Lord spoken by Jeremiah is being fulfilled here. There are two main possibilities. Jeremiah predicted a seventy-year exile

(Jer. 25:11 and Jer. 29:10). 'Seventy years' there could be taken to mean a precise number of years or, more probably, to refer more generally to the idea of a generation.[1] The other possibility is that 'the word of the Lord spoken by Jeremiah' refers to the prophet's broader message that the Lord is sovereign over all earthly kings. Whichever route seems preferable the outcome and application is the same. God is acting sovereignly in history to faithfully keep to His word.

We are not told exactly *how* the Lord moved the heart of Cyrus. It seems likely though that Daniel was a cog in the wheel. This pagan king had clearly learnt a lot about Daniel's God from knowing Daniel over many years and not least from seeing the Lord rescue Daniel from the lions (see Dan. 6:25-28). This might explain some of the highly specific covenant language of the edict in Ezra 1.

The proclamation
Having introduced the context of the king's proclamation, the author then records the proclamation itself (or more probably a truncated form of it). This proclamation is surprising on a number of levels.

---

1. Many readers like to leap to the prediction of a seventy-year exile made in Jeremiah 25:11 or Jeremiah 29:10. Taking such a specific fulfilment is problematic, however, as cursory examination of the dates will show:

▪ Exile	597 B.C.
▪ Destruction of temple	586 B.C.
▪ First return (Ezra 1)	538 B.C.
▪ Completion of temple (Ezra 6)	516 B.C.

The only seventy-year gap is between the destruction of the temple and its rebuilding. However, the Jeremiah passages (unlike, say, Ezekiel) do not associate exile and return with the temple project. Rather they are expressed in terms of Babylonian rule – making the more likely contenders for dates 597 and 538 B.C. – a gap of sixty-one years.

First, it is remarkable that it is given *at all*. Persian King Cyrus is introducing a new policy here. It is a policy which is the exact opposite of the policy of the Babylonian kings who ruled before him. Babylonian policy had been to gather conquered exiles to Babylon out of their various lands so that they could be controlled and mastered. Politically this made a lot of sense. But now new King Cyrus was telling these exiles living in Babylon to return to their homeland and rebuild their place of worship. On the face of it this seems a highly improbable decree and in the past the historical accuracy of Ezra 1 was widely questioned by critical scholars. All this changed, however, with the discovery of the Cyrus Cylinder in 1879.[2] This clay cylinder contains an edict from King Cyrus. It is more general than Ezra 1 – referring to all peoples and exiles. However, the message is the same: exiles may return and rebuild their temples. This ancient document is of such significance that a copy is lodged in the foyer of the United Nations. The original is on display in The British Museum.

The second surprise about Cyrus' proclamation is the clear focus on temple rebuilding. This again sounds unlikely on first reading. But the Cyrus Cylinder helps us here too. It makes clear that Cyrus believed that the way to seal his kingship was for prayers and offerings to be made in the houses of the various regional gods. It seems that Cyrus was a religious pluralist who wanted to try and keep in with every available god. Be that as it may, the focus in Ezra 1 is on the rebuilding of one temple only – that of

---

2. This is such an important biblical archaeological find that I have included a little more detail in Appendix 1.

'The Lord, the God of heaven.' This temple rebuilding will be the focus of the first half of the book.

The third surprise about this proclamation is that the pagan neighbours of these exiled Jews are to help pay for the whole enterprise (v. 4). There are clear echoes of the Exodus from Egypt here when God's people walked out of slavery carrying rich gifts from the Egyptians. It is not going too far to call the events in Ezra a second Exodus. The people leave with the king's blessing and their neighbours' generosity (v. 4). In the events of this chapter we see not only God's sovereignty and His faithfulness but His abundant generosity too. Indeed, we later discover even greater signs of God's generosity to His people. As we read on we find that Cyrus intended that all the temple rebuilding work should be funded by his own government (6:4).

Overall, we as readers need to feel the shock of this unexpected proclamation. It needs to take our breath away. The Jerusalem temple was central to God's covenant with His people and in the extraordinary events of Ezra 1, God is at work to restore it.

God and His people (1:5-11)

In verse 5 the focus switches from Cyrus to the people of God. Here again we see the sovereign control of the Lord over human hearts. A large number of the people of God (42,360 according to 2:64) obey the stirring of God in their hearts and take action in response to the king's command. Neighbours too respond to Cyrus' decree and help the returning Jews with a generosity that echoes the Exodus (compare v. 6 with Exod. 12:36). There are many remarkable things in this chapter not least that God's people should be willing to uproot from their settled existence in Babylon and set off back to the ruins of Israel.

As we read on there is a further turn-up for the books; Cyrus reappears and produces all the contents of the temple treasury that his Babylonian predecessors stole (see 2 Chron. 36:7, 18). Nebuchadnezzar had installed these in the temple of his Babylonian god, believing that the God of Israel had been defeated. Their return now shows how complete the reversal is; despite appearances to the contrary, the God of Israel is far from defeated!

The author notes that these items were counted out to Sheshbazzar, the prince of Judah (v. 8) and then provides an inventory of them (vv. 9-10). His aim is to confirm to us that not one of these precious items is missing. All are returned to the leader of God's people and taken back to Jerusalem (v. 11). The sovereign hand of God is seen in the delicious details of the text here; He is restoring Israel back to her home, her temple and her worship.

Two further textual comments are worth making. First, the precise identity of Sheshbazzar is uncertain. This 'prince of Judah' is mentioned twice more in Ezra. In 5:14 we learn that he was appointed as governor by Cyrus and in 5:16, that he laid the foundations of the Jerusalem temple. Some have wondered if Sheshbazzar is the Babylonian name of Zerubbabel, the Jewish leader who takes centre stage after chapter 1. (We know that Jews in exile sometimes took Babylonian names; Daniel, for example, took the Babylonian name, Belteshazzar.) But that seems unlikely to be the case here. Sheshbazzar is a Babylonian name but Zerubbabel is also a non-Jewish name. Other suggestions for Sheshbazzar's identity have been made but these too are very uncertain. What we

can say is that Sheshbazzar was almost certainly known
to Ezra's original readers and was significant enough to
verify the count – that is what matters and the purpose of
his inclusion.

A second issue arises over the numbers. The list
appears not to add up. If the inventory is totalled it comes
to 2,499 articles, not the 5,400 of verse 11. Probably the
best solution to this discrepancy is to assume that the
total number of items was 5,400 of which 2,499 were
significant enough to be listed separately.

From text to message

Ezra 1 is a colourful passage containing a number of surprises and shocks. That any Jews should want to return
to a broken down home is astounding. They have made
their home in Babylon (see Jer. 29:4-7). That a pagan king
should be behind the exodus is even more incredible.
Our preaching or teaching of this chapter should convey
this astonishment and in so doing we will magnify the
sovereignty and faithfulness of God. When we see how
unlikely these events are, humanly speaking, the arm of
the Lord is seen to be stronger still.

Getting the message clear: the theme

The theme of the passage is God sovereignly restoring His
people to worship Him (This is the end purpose of rebuilding the physical temple.).

Getting the message clear: the aim

We want our hearers to see the sovereign hand of the Lord
making it possible for people to come to Him in worship.
Here in Ezra we see a foreshadowing of our salvation in
Christ. The sovereign hand of God has made it possible

through Christ's death and resurrection for us also to come to Him in worship. There too God worked sovereignly even in those who rejected Him to bring about His good purposes. Moreover, there is an abundance in the gift of Christ which is foreshadowed in some way in the details of this passage. The preacher who can capture the wonder of what God does in Ezra 1 will find a natural path to encourage his hearers to see the wonder of what God does in Christ in *the* salvation event of the cross.

This seems the most natural and appropriate way to preach Christ from Ezra 1. There are other possibilities such as the continuity of the princely line but this is a minor matter in the passage. It seems best to major on the major theme of the passage in looking for the line to Christ.

A way in

The events of Ezra 1 are extraordinary and unlikely. An introduction which helps listeners grasp this will set the teaching up well. This could be an historical approach which shows (before the discovery of the Cyrus Cylinder) just how unlikely it all seemed. Alternatively, it would be possible to paint a picture of immigrants seventy years on – say to the USA. Millions of people passed through Ellis Island Immigration Centre and settled in various parts of the USA. They might still feel some nostalgia about their homelands, but as they settled down in the US and raised families of their own the idea that they would uproot and return to lands they could hardly remember would seem utterly preposterous.

Ideas for application

- A key theme in this chapter is the sovereignty of God. Primarily, God's sovereignty is seen in bringing about the salvation of His people from slavery in exile. There is a direct line from here to God's sovereignty over the saving cross of Christ. In texts such as Acts 2:23 we are told explicitly that Jesus' death 'was according to God's set purpose and foreknowledge'. However, the sovereignty of God in the big things (salvation) is a clear indication of the power of God in *all* things. God's sovereignty is a key theme in the whole book of Ezra. This is a truth that should both humble us (when things are going well, it is God who is responsible) and encourage us (when things are going badly, God is still on His throne).

- God's sovereign actions in Ezra display not only His saving power but also the abundance of His generosity to His people. God moves Cyrus to shower blessings on God's people. He returns the temple treasures, commands people of all lands to give presents to the departing Jews and pays for the building programme himself. We are seeing something here about the nature of God's sovereign rule. There are no half measures or stingy left-overs but only the abundant generosity of the One who gives all things for the good of His people, even giving His Son.

- The sovereign actions of God in Ezra also express God's commitment to keep His word. This is made explicit in verse 1 as we have seen. Christians should have confidence that the One who has always kept His word always will.

- Ezra 1 makes clear that rebuilding God's temple is to be the first priority of God's returning people.

Nehemiah's work to rebuild the walls of Jerusalem came later. This order shows us that the worship of God in His appointed way is to come before all things. The same is true today.

- The return of the temple articles – carefully counted out – is evidence that the God of Israel has not been defeated despite apparent evidence to the contrary in the time of the exile.

Suggestions for preaching

Sermon 1

Any sermon on Ezra 1 needs to set the scene in such a way that the unexpectedness of the chapter's events is conveyed clearly. This will help the hearers appreciate more fully the wonder of God's sovereignty in bringing about the return from exile. It is this sovereignty of God in saving His people that needs to be the main focus of the sermon as it is so clearly the main theme of the passage.

- **God is unfailingly faithful to His word (v. 1).** It is God's faithfulness to His word which prompts His sovereign action. Moreover, God's past faithfulness is a measure of His future faithfulness. Not one of His promises has ever failed nor ever will.

- **God is abundantly sovereign in His salvation (vv. 2-11).** His faithfulness translates into sovereign action both in the pagan king and in His people. This picture gives us confidence that the ways that God works in the world, though sometimes unseen, will nevertheless bring about His gracious purposes and ultimately His generous salvation in Christ Jesus.

Sermon 2

It is possible to combine chapter 1 with chapter 2 into one teaching passage (especially for a Bible study). We will look at how that might be done in the next chapter.

Suggestions for teaching

Questions to help understand the passage

1. How had the Israelites got to this point? Briefly review 2 Chronicles 36.

2. What word had Jeremiah spoken (v. 1)? Look up Jeremiah 29:10 for a specific word or Jeremiah 33:1-11 for a more general prophecy.

3. What is the key phrase which makes clear that God is behind all the events of chapter 1?

4. Why should we be surprised by what takes place in this chapter?

5. Why is the focus on restoring the temple rather than rebuilding the city, restoring the throne or resettling the land?

6. What is the point of listing the treasury items that are returned in verses 9-10?

Questions to help apply the passage

1. How does reflecting on the faithfulness of God *in the past* help us think about His faithfulness in the future?

2. What key promises of God are yet to be fulfilled?

3. What is the supreme event that displays God's sovereign rule and faithfulness? How?

4. How does God's sovereignty keep us humble when things go well? Think of church and personal examples.

5. How does God's sovereignty keep us encouraged when things go badly?

6. How is the abundant provision of God seen in the lives of Christians today? Make sure your answers work in a variety of contexts – for example, in the lives of persecuted believers.

2. The people at their best (Ezra 2:1-70)

This is a record of the names of the exiles who returned to rebuild the temple. It is divided into different sections according to family name, geographical location and temple jobs. Once they are back at the temple site in Jerusalem the Jews give generous offerings to pay for the rebuilding and then disperse to settle in their own towns.

Introduction

Chapter 2 is a key record in the life of the people of God; not only does it have a prominent place in Ezra but the entire chapter is also repeated in Nehemiah (Neh. 7:6-73). Nehemiah himself makes it clear that this is an official court record of the returning exiles (Neh. 7:5). Given that these people are commanded to rebuild the temple by King Cyrus and that costly treasure is committed to their care we should not be surprised that their names are so carefully recorded.

It is essential, however, to reflect on how this passage works as Scripture. It is tempting to pass over such passages in a preaching or teaching programme; they hardly seem at first sight to be profitable ground for an expository sermon or stimulating Bible study. However, the wise preacher or teacher will not overlook Ezra 2. There are a number of good reasons for paying careful attention to this chapter as we teach through this Bible book.

First, as we shall see the content of the chapter is more than a list of names and numbers. Like other parts of the book, this section is written carefully to convey meaning as well as information. It is not simply an early telephone directory.

Second, overlooking such passages conveys the wrong message to congregations. If we do not teach this chapter we give the impression that this part of God's word is somehow excluded from the Bible's self-assertion that 'All Scripture is breathed out by God and useful...' (2 Tim. 3:16, italics added). We want instead to show our hearers that God is speaking in all of Scripture and that we are keen to listen to what He wants to say. This is fundamental to our expository method and convictions and so including teaching on Ezra 2 does, in itself, convey an important and helpful message to our congregations.

To see how this passage functions it is useful to think how it might have been received by its first hearers. We could imagine a post-exilic Jewish family listening to the Scriptures being read and their excitement when they hear their family name or town. 'Dad', cries the enthusiastic youngster, 'that's Great-Grandad!' Recognising such personal links would have been of more than just passing interest to these first hearers. It would have been a positive encouragement to be faithful to the Lord, just as their ancestors had been. Those listed in Ezra 2 are a record of the people of God at their best. Those named in this chapter responded obediently to God and to the command of the king. They wanted to get things right. The first hearers might well have looked back to these faithful and honourable ancestors and been challenged to keep their own families following in their footsteps.

One question many have is whether we can really read out such a passage in church. Won't it just take too long? Won't the names be too hard to pronounce? Reading Ezra

2 word for word with numbers 'spelled' out takes only about five minutes. This is time well spent in my view not least because it shows our reverence for all of Scripture. Perhaps the pronunciation of the names is also daunting? The passage certainly requires a very confident reader!

Listening to the text

Context and structure

Chapter 2 essentially belongs with chapter 1. It is a list of those whose 'hearts God had moved' (1:5). The form and ordering of the list show us the author's concerns and purpose.

First, we are introduced to the leaders or heads of families (v. 2). Then there follows two lists of Israelites; one list groups the people by family name (vv. 3-20) then a second list groups them by family town (vv. 21-35).

From verse 36 onwards, the focus shifts to those who would serve in the temple, once it was rebuilt. Restoring worship within this rebuilt temple would require priests, Levites, musicians, and a number of other temple servants. The author lists people in all these different groups. Finally, we have a summary total of all who returned (vv. 64-67) followed by a description of a spontaneous offering by heads of families towards the cost of the rebuilding (vv. 68-69). So the structure of the list is this:

- Listing the leaders (2:1-2)

- Listing the people (2:3-35)

- Listing the temple workers (2:36-63)

- A summary of those whose hearts God had moved (2:64-70)

This list also appears in Nehemiah 7, a fact that underlines the importance and significance ascribed to this record of faithful Jews. There are a few minor differences between the lists. Possible explanations for these differences are explored in more detail in Appendix 2.

Working through the text

Listing the leaders (2:1-2)

The first group we meet are almost certainly the key leaders in the returning community. We can surmise this from the way the list is headed by Zerubbabel and Jeshua[3] who take the lead on a number of occasions in the rest of the book.

Zerubbabel is the son of Shealtiel (5:2), himself a son of King Jehoiachin and a grandson of Jehoiakim. Shealtiel and Jehoiachin (also called Jeconiah) both appear in the Matthew genealogy. It seems that the line of David is being maintained here. That is certainly the way that the gospel writer Matthew sees it.

Alongside Zerubbabel is the High Priest, Joshua, (called Jeshua in some versions). This is Joshua son of Jozadak (Ezra 5:2), not Joshua son of Nun, Moses' successor from many generations before. We don't know so much about this Joshua's pedigree but he was clearly a priest (2:36), and he and Zerubbabel formed a strong leadership alliance. They are generally spoken of together in the book of Ezra (2:2, 3:2, 8, 4:3, 5:2) and are directly addressed in the prophecies of both Haggai (1:1) and Zechariah (3:1 and 4:6).

This strong duo is accompanied by nine others listed in verse 2. There are some names which are familiar to us in

---

3. An alternative way to spell the name Joshua.

this leadership list but these are almost certainly not the same characters we know from other stories. We can tell this from looking at the dates of different Bible events.

Listing the people (2:3-35)

Each line in Hebrew begins the same way: 'the sons of...' (see ESV). But the NIV rightly splits the list into two with verses 3-20 represented as families and verses 21-35 as places. Such a split is not unexpected. In earlier times every family had a portion of the promised land as an inheritance which was passed down the generations. Families were identified by the land they possessed. But as Judah was attacked again and again before the exile, lands were lost and the country was reduced in size to a city state. Because of this, some of the exiled families would have been identified by family name rather than by their home town or area. Other families could still be identified by their area of land. Some might have left their territory relatively recently or their territory might have been near enough to Jerusalem to be incorporated with it. Some home towns were probably of such significance that they would never be forgotten (Bethlehem almost certainly ticks that box). Listing some of the returning Jews by family name and others by family territory shows the great care that was taken over this record. The author wants to correctly identify and include all the men who returned. There is also an order in the list which is not seen by modern readers. The geographic places are not listed in a random fashion but broadly trace a path around the points of the compass.

There is precision in the actual counting too. These are precise records of those who returned, those whose hearts were moved and whose inclusion in the list calls forth 'respect and gratitude'.[4] That would surely have been the response of Ezra's first Jewish readers and it should be ours today too.

Listing the temple workers (2:36-63)

Next comes a list of priests. Priests came from the tribe of Levi and so were a part of the Israelite community. Any returning group would naturally include priests.

But there is more than simple tribe-counting going on here. The focus of this return to Jerusalem has been made very clear in chapter 1: the people of God are to rebuild the temple so that they can worship the Lord. The structure of the list of returnees shows a clear appreciation of this focus. So the chapter contains lists of the various groups who would be needed to make temple worship possible. In this record there are not only lists of priests but also:

- Levites (v. 40) – a general grouping who would have had some temple duties (see 1 Chron. 23)

- Musicians (v. 41) (see 1 Chron. 25)

- Gatekeepers (v. 42) – these would be men of trust who stood guard (see 1 Chron. 9.21-24 and 1 Chron. 26)

- Temple servants (v. 43)

- Descendants of the servants of Solomon (v. 55) – we are not sure of the exact function of this group though the way they are grouped together with the

4. Carson, D. A., *For the love of God*, vol. 2 (Nottingham, UK: IVP Books, 1998), entry for January 2.

Temple servants in v. 58 suggests that their role was
some kind of work in the temple or temple precinct.

There is a clear intended focus here. Each specific group
is expressly defined in relation to its work at the temple.
The primary aim of the return was to restore the worship
activities of the temple. This aim is reflected clearly and
positively in the ordering of these lists.

But this focus is also reflected in the groupings which
do *not* appear in this record. The Israelites are returning to
rebuild the temple. But where are the lists of stonemasons,
artisans, weavers, metal workers and so on? Given that the
building project is so significant and will take so long, they
are noticeable by their absence.

The answer of course is that these skilled people *are*
here amongst the families who return but they are not
listed separately. The author wants us to see beyond what
the building will *be* to what it will be *for*. Nothing less than
the pure worship of the Lord is at stake and so the authors
are at pains to point out those who are needed to make it
happen. (There will be a similar focus in 8:15 during the
second return.)

At the end of the lists of specific groups there is a record
of those who wanted to return to Jerusalem but could not
prove their lineage. Some could not prove their lineage as
Israelites (vv. 59-60). Others could not prove their lineage
as priests (vv. 61-63). We may wonder why this matter is
included. It seems that the people and priests listed here
did return with the rest of the Israelites. There is also no
indication as we read on that these priests were found to
be imposters. The issue is rather that they cannot *prove*

their priesthood and so for the moment it is better for them not to serve.

This regulation is not to be permanent. Once the Israelites are back in situ and things are operating normally again then the 'Urim and Thummim' can be used to determine these people's claim to proper lineage. Presumably if this is confirmed then they will be reinstated in the list.

What is going on here? This is Israel at her best and so it is not surprising to see a right concern for purity. As we will see in chapter 3 this is a people who are careful to keep all the Lord's commands and everything that is written in the Law (3:2). The concern for purity expressed in these verses is symptomatic of that concern. These people want to get things right this time. So, far from being some kind of racial discrimination, these verses describe a passion for purity and precise obedience to God's law which will sadly fade away once they are established back in the land.

Those whose hearts God had moved (2:64-70)

Finally, we get a total number of returnees: 42,360 as well as slaves (from other nations), singers (presumably non-Israelite choristers) and animals. This is quite a camel train. The journey from Babylon to Jerusalem is some nine hundred miles (a rather roundabout route but there is no direct journey possible due west from Babylon). Later in the book this journey takes three and half months (7:8) although that is almost certainly record-breaking. It's also a journey on foot. The horses, mules, camels and donkeys would almost certainly be mostly pack animals.

So here are 42,360 of Israel's finest but the story has not quite finished. When the exiles crest the brow of the hill and see the task ahead of them (the rebuilding of the house of the Lord; notice, not the rebuilding of the city or the walls) they immediately dip into their pockets (v. 68). This freewill offering may be partly handing on the sums that they had been given back in Babylon (1:4, 6) or it may be gifts in addition to this. Either way these offerings are presented as being both spontaneous and in proportion to individual wealth (v. 69). The amount raised here is extraordinary. The gold weighs half a metric ton. The silver almost three tons. These are incredible sums. The staggering generosity of these gifts would have been obvious to the first hearers.

The chapter ends with returned exiles beginning to live once again in their promised land (v. 70). This conclusion is entirely appropriate. They're back! They're ready! What now? The work to rebuild the temple and restore its worship can begin.

From text to message

Two approaches are possible here. One is to preach chapters 1 and 2 together as one teaching unit. The other is to take chapter 2 as a separate, standalone unit. In each case the purpose of the chapter 2 is the same – it is to show us the people whose hearts God moved. This is Israel at her best. If preached with chapter 1, which stresses the faithful and sovereign rule of God, then chapter 2 will show us the kind of people who live happily under this rule. If chapter 2 is preached as a separate unit then that link with God's sovereignty may receive less attention. But the chapter will still show us the priorities and obedience which characterise those whose hearts God has moved.

Getting the message clear: the theme
Israel at her best delights in the Law and longs to worship her God.

Getting the message clear: the aim
What does a good man or woman of God look like? What characterises them? Here are those whose hearts God moved and we see them at their best. There is much to learn. But we need to see Israel first through the lens of Christ. As we move to the New Covenant we realise that the true Israelite is not you or me but Jesus Christ, the firstborn called out of Egypt. On that basis, when we see Israel at her best we are to see a reflection of the character and perfection of Jesus.

There are lessons for us to learn here and examples to follow but these apply to us inasmuch as they first describe Christ and point us to Him. In Christ's perfect obedience we find a description of the righteousness which is ours in Christ through His sacrifice for us. In His obedience we also see a model for us to follow as He empowers us to live differently.

A way in
If preaching this unit separately it would be possible to introduce the idea that a list of names can capture the imagination. For example, imagine visiting a war memorial. I have recently done this myself. The memorial in question (Thiepval in northern France) contains the names of all the Commonwealth soldiers who died in the Battle of the Somme but whose bodies were never found. It is moving experience to read the names recorded there. The tendency of everyone who visits is to search for their own name.

Even if they do not know of relatives who died in the battle people are still drawn to read the names and look for those which are familiar. There is a sense of awe and wonder too. This illustration only goes so far. Many of those who died in that war had no choice in the matter; they were conscripts. Yet their names are displayed with honour and glory. How much more glorious the list of those whose hearts God moved! And how much more there is to this list in Ezra 2 than just name and rank! For here we find, embedded in this record, something of the story and purposes of these people of God.

Ideas for application

- Aside from the wonder of God's sovereignty in moving 42,360 people we also learn something about them from this list. There is a clear sense of blessing from God. Here are the ones He had chosen and set His favour upon. They are listed here for no other reason; there was nothing intrinsically good about them; they were simply objects of the Lord's affection. God had chosen to move their hearts and now they were on their way to His promised land.

- The list also highlights purpose. Under God, what counts to these men and women is the re-establishment of worship at the temple. It's almost as though the building project (great though that will be) is just a staging post. It is the proper operation of the Levitical sacrifices that is the end in mind. They are returning to Jerusalem to worship God.

- The strange interlude about proving lineage also teaches us about a concern for purity. At this stage (even though this will later disappear) the people of God are eager to get things right. They know why they were exiled and they are keen to avoid a repeat of that disobedience.

- The extraordinary generosity that we see in the freewill offering also marks out the people of God at their best.

- We see all of these characteristics in Christ Jesus Himself, the true Israelite. He too was chosen by God for a great purpose. He too made true worship possible. His high priestly ministry opened up the way to the Father: that was why He came. In order to offer Himself, He perfectly kept the Law in a way that these Israelites never ultimately could. And His sacrifice is the perfect measure of generosity on which all Christian giving is modelled. As we see Israel at her best we are to look beyond her to see perfect Jesus and remember what it means to be in Him. Remarkably, those who follow Him will also find their names in a list, later called 'The Lamb's book of life' (Rev. 13:8).

Suggestions for preaching

Sermon 1

The first way to preach Ezra 2 is together with Ezra 1 in a combined sermon. There would be a lot of material here but there is a natural connection between these two chapters. God is revealed in chapter 1 as the faithful and sovereign One who chooses to move the hearts of His people to obey

Him. Then in chapter 2 we see how those who have been chosen respond in terms of their focus, their purity and their generosity. It might be harder in this sermon to make a link to Christ (not least because of time pressures) but it is essential that we do if we are to avoid calling people to a kind of works-based religion.

Sermon 2

Alternatively, a sermon just on chapter 2 might pick up on how the list answers the question – what behaviour and priorities are seen in people whose hearts God has moved?

- **A people with a purpose: worship.** Both explicitly (in what is there) and implicitly (in what is omitted) it is clear that these people are returning to Jerusalem with the aim of seeing the temple worship restored and functioning as it should. There is no mention here of stones, walls or temple building – that will all come later. What comes first in their priorities is a living relationship with the God who is sovereign.

- **A people with a focus: purity.** There is a key focus in the text on getting things right. Not only are all the temple operations represented in the way the list is ordered but, more explicitly, those who cannot prove their lineage cannot serve as priests just yet. The Law must be observed.

- **A people with an attitude: generosity.** The stunning giving of those returning is breath-taking. No doubt the project is an expensive one but we later discover that Cyrus is paying for it anyway (6:4). These gifts seem to be over and above what

may have been needed and reflect the gratitude
that the people have towards God.

In all of this Israel at her best shows us Christ and draws
us to Him. He is the perfect and true Israelite and these
are marks of His ministry and life in saving us. They are
marks too of what it therefore means to live in Him.

Suggestions for teaching

Questions to help understand the passage

1. Read through the list of names together. What do
   you think the author wants you to know about these
   names? Look for clues and emphases.

2. Given that they are coming back to rebuild the
   temple, what jobs are missing from the list? Why
   do you suppose that is?

3. Why do we need to know about those who cannot
   prove their lineage (vv. 60-63)?

4. Given that Cyrus is paying for this building (see 6:4),
   what do you suppose the offering in vv. 68-69 is all
   about?

Questions to help apply the passage

1. What does this passage teach us about the response
   of those whose hearts God has moved?

2. How do these Israelites – at their best – show us the
   character and life of Jesus? Try to think of specific
   examples and New Testament references.

3. How does thinking about Jesus from this passage help us draw good lessons for us today? What are they?

4. What distractions that take our eyes from the wholehearted worship of the living God do churches face?

5. Why do you think we lack concern for purity and generosity? What can we do to recover a right response in these areas?

3. First things first (Ezra 3:1-6)

The returned Jews re-gather in Jerusalem led by Joshua the priest and Zerubbabel the descendant of David. Before they begin rebuilding the temple itself the Jews rebuild the altar. They then begin to offer burnt offerings on the altar and begin to celebrate the Jewish feasts, notably the Feast of Tabernacles.

Introduction

At first glance this short section of chapter 3 does not seem of great interest or significance. However, as I hope to show, nothing could be further from the truth. The clue to understanding this section and bringing it to life is within the text itself, for we are told that 'they began to offer burnt offerings to the Lord, though the foundation of the Lord's temple had not yet been laid' (3:6). This hermeneutical key opens up the passage to us. There is something to be done before the building work can even be started.

The returning exiles have come back at the instruction of the king to rebuild the temple (1:2). Moreover, the Lord has put it into their hearts to rebuild the temple (1:5), and the entire focus of chapter 2 (as we have seen) is on the worship that will one day be offered at the reconstructed house of God. Therefore it is significant that the very first thing they do on their return is build an altar and offer sacrifices rather than start work on the temple building itself. It is this 'surprise' that 3:6 highlights and which opens up the main lines of application.

Listening to the text

Context and structure

It appears – at first glance – that 3:1-6 belongs best with the rest of chapter 3, which contains the rest of the account of the temple rebuilding work. Chapter 2 lists those who have returned and now chapter 3 describes what the returnees actually *did*. Chapter 3 can be preached as an entity and I will suggest a way of doing that in the next chapter.

However, 3:1-6 probably more naturally belongs with chapter 2 especially that chapter's latter verses. There we saw the people of God at their best diligently obeying the Law of the Lord and responding to His gracious sovereign work in their hearts with awesome generosity. The connection between the end of chapter 2 and the beginning of chapter 3 is made clear by the repeated phrase 'settled in their towns' in 2:70 and 3:1.

The first part of chapter 3 continues the theme of chapter 2 – here are the people of God at their best striving to keep the law (a repeated theme) with a particular focus on burnt offerings and festival observance. All this appears to be a necessary precursor to even starting any building work. The NIV splits the passage after verse 6 whilst the ESV makes the divide after verse 7. It seems though that the end of verse 6 is the more natural break point. This verse closes and summarises the description of building the altar first so that sacrifices could begin.

There are no natural divisions within verses 1-6 but we can draw out the main themes of this passage as we work through the text. In this section we see:

- The gathering of the nation

- The leadership of the people

- The obedience to the Law

- The offerings and festivals

Working through the text

This is not a particularly complex passage but there is one difficult exegetical question (regarding whether in verse 3 the people rebuilt the altar *because of* fear or *in spite of* it) and there are also some important indicators that need to be identified.

The gathering of the nation

The first verse of chapter 3 picks up where chapter 2 left off. There we learnt that the people of God 'settled in their towns'; now the narrative uses the same phrase to indicate that the people re-gather at the temple after they had dispersed to their home towns. This is an important detail. The assembly of the people 'as one man' to begin the work would have been less extraordinary if it had happened at precisely the moment that all the Israelites first arrived at the temple (i.e. chronologically at 2:68) immediately after their journey together from Babylon.

Now, however, the people have dispersed. They have gone back 'home' – even though home meant towns and cities that would have been at least partially still in ruins.[5] Faced with the scale of the task of rebuilding their own houses it is doubly remarkable that the people should heed the call to gather together to rebuild the house of God and celebrate His festivals. Of course, the Law required

---

5. The apocryphal account softens the blow. In 1 Esdras 5:46, the Israelites are recorded as settling in Jerusalem itself. The gathering of chapter 3 is not nearly so remarkable on this basis.

them to gather together – for example, celebrating the Feast of Tabernacles (3:4) was a key Mosaic instruction (see Lev. 23:33-43); all men were called to assemble to celebrate it (see also Exod. 34:23). But given the state of their home towns after the exile it would have been easy for God's people to have put other concerns first.

The repeated mention of the people's settlement in their towns thus amplifies the remarkable nature of their assembling again 'as one man.' That phrase is pregnant: it signifies not just that everyone was there but also that there was a unity of purpose about their gathering. (The phrase will be repeated in Neh. 8:1.)

This unity of purpose is a characteristic of the people at their best and one which sadly is soon lost. By chapter 4 opposition has divided the nation and we know from the preaching of Haggai that the Israelites later became more interested in their own personal building projects than those of the Lord. Indeed, by the end of the book of Ezra the people's desire to pursue their own personal desires and goals rather than God's has taken an extreme hold. Shockingly, the intermarriage with pagans that marked their original apostasy was back in vogue again. For now, however, we are to think well of these exiles. They are of one mind; perhaps we should not be surprised since it is a mind that the Lord Himself has given to them (1:5).

The leadership of the people

In 3:2 we see Joshua and Zerubbabel (first mentioned in 2:2) providing spiritual and civil leadership for the nation. This dynamic leadership duo takes the lead together on a number of occasions in Ezra. Joshua was a priest whose lineage is briefly described ('son of Jozadak'), possibly to distinguish him from any other Joshua (a common enough name). It may also be to reinforce his priestly credentials, given the uncertainty about the lineage of some priests in 2:62.

Joshua is accompanied by Zerubbabel, son of Shealtiel, who is distinguished from the priests (3:2). Although never known by a particular leadership title Zerubbabel appears to have been a civic leader of some kind, possibly fulfilling a Nehemiah-type role as governor of the people. This would have been entirely appropriate as he was the direct descendant of David through his father Shealtiel, himself the son of Jeconiah (Matt. 1:12, compare 1 Chron. 3:16). Once the temple building programme begins and opposition comes, Zerubbabel is always named first whenever the duo is mentioned. This probably indicates that he had the first place in the leadership team. Here in 3:2 he almost certainly comes second because of the nature of what is about to take place: priestly sacrifices in keeping with the Law.

The leadership team's first act is to build the 'altar of the God of Israel to sacrifice burnt offerings on it.' This building priority is presented as surprising for two reasons. First, it happens 'despite their fear of the peoples around them' (v.3). This little phrase requires some explanation. The Hebrew conjunction *ki* which the NIV translates as 'despite' can also be translated 'for,' as it is in the ESV. This would completely change the meaning of the sentence. In the first case, the building of the altar would happen *despite* the opposition and in the second, *because* of the opposition. These two different translations could lead to quite different applications. Given the context of the surrounding sections though, the NIV reading seems much more likely: this first part of Ezra seems to be showing us the people of God at their best in a whole range of ways. We know from chapter

4 that those living around them did try to intimidate these Jews into giving up their building work (4:4). But we also see that the leaders of Israel did not give up despite this opposition. It would clearly go against the grain of these first chapters therefore to interpret 3:3 as describing the people of God giving way to intimidation. Nothing else in the text suggests this. In fact, the whole section of 3:1-6 speaks rather of the Israelites' absolute commitment to please God above all other concerns. Taking all this together the NIV reading seems clearly preferable.

The priority of the altar

The building work on the altar is deliberately identified as taking place before the foundation of the temple is laid (v. 6). The altar was not actually *in* the temple of course. It was, however, in the temple courts, close to the temple – and therefore this construction of the altar before the temple (particularly when the Israelites had been instructed to return and build the temple) is striking and significant. The altar was the place where offerings were made – and in this chapter the focus is very clearly on burnt offerings (repeated five times). Burnt offerings were atonement sin offerings (see Lev. 1:4) – not the annual Day of Atonement offering but rather the regular daily reminders of sin and its need to be dealt with.

Thus the building of the altar first, before the rest of the work, depicted the importance and need for the whole Israelite community to be right with God before they could even begin to contemplate actually building the temple itself.

To an outsider looking on this would probably have appeared topsy-turvy. In architectural terms it would be like landscaping your garden before building the main house. However, in spiritual terms it makes complete sense. The people of God understood that they had been exiled precisely because they had not loved the Lord their God with all their heart, mind and strength. As they returned to rebuild, it seems that they fully comprehended that this vertical relationship with their Redeemer took priority over everything else – even the building of a temple to His name.

The obedience to the Law

There is a clear commitment to keeping the Law of the Lord throughout this passage. As well as direct references to Law-keeping (for example, the many references to burnt offerings) the passage is also replete with phrases which indirectly make much of this Law-keeping attitude. Chief among these is the identification of the Law as being the Law of 'Moses, the man of God.' This is an unusual title but significantly it links Moses to the role of prophet. 'The man of God' is a title shared by Samuel (1 Sam. 9:6), Elijah (1 Kings 17:18) and Elisha (2 Kings 4:7) as well as numerous unnamed prophets. On the two occasions it is used of Moses, both are about the prophetic word being spoken (the national blessing of Deut. 33:1 and the anointing of his successor reported in Josh. 14:6). Here then we are meant to think of the Law, not only in its role of calling people to obedience, but also in its prophetic role – pointing forward to the better future God had planned.

The people's obedience is presented as comprehensive. This is captured in repeated phrases such as 'in accordance with', 'required', 'prescribed' and 'appointed.' We are left in no doubt (if there was any left after chapter 2) that the people of God here are wholly committed to keeping the

word of the Lord as expressed in the Law of Moses. There
is to be no repeat of the folly that led them into exile.

The offerings and festivals

Finally, this obedience is seen in the offerings and festivals. From the beginning of the seventh month the daily
burnt offerings are re-established (3:6). The Festival of
Tabernacles is celebrated (3:4) and then all the other
sacred festivals and sacrifices are re-instated (3:5).

Tabernacles is the only festival specifically mentioned
and it is also the first festival the people celebrate. This is
notable as there were two other festivals (Trumpets and
the Day of Atonement) that came before Tabernacles in
this seventh month. We may wonder why the people did
not begin with these, especially given their evident desire
here to carefully obey the Law.

It may be that what happens here shows us a number
of significant spiritual truths and the people's recognition
of them.

First, this rebuilt temple was going to be inadequate
and incomplete. The Festival of Trumpets, which began on
the first day of the seventh month, comprised ten days of
preparation for the Day of Atonement which took place on
the tenth day (Lev. 23). These two festivals went together
and both are omitted here. It seems likely that this was
because the Day of Atonement could not be properly
celebrated without an actual temple and in particular
without the ark of the covenant (see Lev. 16) which the
people no longer possessed. When the building work was
finished, there would be a rebuilt temple but there would
still be no ark and so the glory of God would never reside in
this temple, as it did in the former one. (When this temple

is completed in Chapter 6, God's glory does not descend on it as had happened with the first temple.) The people's inability here to properly celebrate the Day of Atonement should point us forward to Jesus, the perfect and complete temple of God, where God's glory fully dwells and where sins can be fully and finally dealt with.

Secondly, the choice to begin with and to specifically mention the Festival of Tabernacles may show once again that both the people and the author saw links between the return from exile and the first Exodus. The Feast of Tabernacles was a vivid reminder of the time God's people lived in temporary shelters in the desert when God brought them out of Egypt (Lev. 23:43). The people in Ezra 3 might have found many echoes of their current situation in this Feast of Tabernacles. They would have been not only thankful to God for bringing them out of captivity, but also aware that they were not yet living in a finished homeland.

From text to message

It would be difficult for a sermon on this passage to follow carefully delineated divisions. The important points are woven together throughout the text. That is not a problem. Expository preaching does not require us to reduce every narrative passage down into three sections or dramatic scenes. Some narratives simply do not work that way. This is one of those passages where a good sermon will focus on the lessons to be drawn and let that guide the form of the sermon rather than trying to impose a structure on a short, dense story.

Getting the message clear: the theme

Israel at her best knows that a living relationship with the Lord God counts before all else.

Getting the message clear: the aim

As before, Israel at her best teaches us about Christ. He is the true Israelite, who counted obedience to His Father above all else. Sent to do the will of the One who sent Him, He set all else aside, securing our eternal salvation by His once for all sin offering. As such, Israel at her best show us Christ in His incarnational glory. However, there is more to this passage than this –Christians are *in Christ* and so we learn from Christ, the true Israelite, about loving the Lord our God with all our heart, soul, mind and strength.

In other words, there are lessons here about how Christ builds the church – His temple – precisely because this is so clearly foreshadowed here. As with many parts of Ezra, there is a rich variety of foreshadowings of Christ here: in gathering people together as one (Eph. 2:11-22), in leadership (Zerubbabel in Matt. 1), in sacrifice as a sin offering (Heb. 10:5-7), in Moses, the Man of God (Heb. 3:1-6) and in Law-keeping. However, though any of these might be legitimate ways to preach Christ, it seems best to go with the main thrust of the passage, which is to present the people of God doing well and living as they ought to live as they get ready to build. There is really nothing negative to say about them here.

A way in

The surprise of building the altar *before* the temple itself would be a great place to start a sermon (3:6). Listeners or group members need to feel the shock of the people choosing to do this first. How are people so far distant from the Law and its seemingly archaic requirements going to feel the force of this surprise? A good introduction will help them feel it – possibly by helping people see the apparent absurdity of, say, fitting out a kitchen before making the walls of the house. Such an illustration is obviously limited and imperfect but it allows the preacher or teacher to pose the question which this passage answers: why would you do that?

I have also started a sermon on this passage with an illustration about IKEA. It is easy to discover their extraordinary sales figures online. They make flat-pack everything! But how do you go about making a temple? No IKEA assembly instructions sheet to help here. However, here's the answer: according to chapter 3 you start with the end. It's the last, finishing piece which gets made first and as we read this passage we come to understand why this topsy-turvy building approach is entirely appropriate.

Ideas for application

- In Christ, the perfect Israelite, God's people find a unity of purpose and action reflected most clearly in their gathering together.

- We understand that our relationship with the holy living God (both individually and corporately) counts before anything else. It is easy to become distracted by all manner of worthy causes (including building projects!), but the word of God helps us keep the main thing the main thing.

- This single-minded focus should not be affected by the seriousness of the situations we face. In fact opposition only increases the need for us to

be vigilant vertically, i.e. in our relationship with
God through Jesus.

- At the heart of our relationship with God is the
  understanding that we are sinners and sacrifice
  for sin needs to be made. There is no way to
  be right with God except through the perfect
  Law-keeper, the true Man of God. Once saved
  we need to make sure we are thankful and
  remember our salvation and how the Lord has
  brought us up out of slavery.

Suggestions for preaching

Sermon 1

At the heart of the passage is the priority of altar-
rebuilding and this needs to shape the sermon as well.
Restoring the altar comes before the temple building but
is not independent of it. Thus a sermon could help people
see how Christ builds His church, His temple – but each
point would need to be rooted in Christ to make sense and
avoid works-type applications.

- **We build with complete unity.** The gospel
  project calls the people together and they act as
  one man. It's not an attitude that can be taken for
  granted as it is later lost. We are joined together
  by a common purpose.

- **We build with right priorities.** We need to see
  the importance of building 'the altar', where sins
  are paid for, first. In Christ we see the cost of our
  salvation through His sacrifice for sins; we see too
  the need always to be mindful of the sin that can

so easily entangle. Only fixing our eyes on Him (Heb. 12.1-2) will allow us to get this right.

- **We build with fearless energy.** Not everyone will respond well to the building of Christ's church and why should they? Apart from Him, they are enemies of God. This opposition should make us more determined to get things right, not less so.

- **We build with joyful obedience.** Obedience cannot earn our salvation (as indeed the people of God found in Ezra). Nevertheless, obedience should be a fruit of salvation, flowing from a thankful heart. Those who are in Christ *want* to keep His royal Law and want to do it joyfully – as the festivals demonstrate.

Sermon 2

If this passage was combined with the previous chapter, the Law-keeping obedience and the priority given to sacrifice found in 3:1-6 would sit as happy partners to the commitment to purity of 2:61-63, and the generosity of 2:68-69. These sections could easily be grouped together. It seems to me that a sermon on burnt offerings or festivals rather misses the thrust of the passage, launching from an idea in the passage that is not its primary focus. If required, this first part of this chapter could be joined together with the remainder of chapter 3 and I will suggest an outline which serves this purpose in the next chapter.

Suggestions for teaching

Questions to help understand the passage

1. What festivals should have been celebrated in the seventh month (quickly review Lev. 23 for a reminder)?

2. Which festival is highlighted here (v. 4) and why do you suppose that is?

3. Read through the passage again. What is emphasised by means of repetition? What do you suppose the author wants us to understand?

4. Why does fear of others (v. 3) not stop the altar building programme?

5. What – primarily – does the author want you to understand about this altar building (see v. 6)?

Questions to help apply the passage

1. How do the Israelites – at their best – show us Christ Jesus in attitude and action?

2. What kind of unity do the people have and how does being in Christ bring that unity today?

3. What do we learn here about the priorities we should have as we serve Christ?

4. What kinds of difficulties might tempt us to lose this single-minded focus (v. 3)? How can we fight against this?

5. What do we learn about sin and sacrifice in this passage? How do we keep these lessons front and centre as we are busy with many worthy projects and initiatives?

4. Joy and sadness (Ezra 3:7-13)

The construction of the main temple is organised and begun, supervised by the Levites. The foundation stone is laid with the appropriate religious ceremony prescribed by King David for the first temple. There is both weeping and joy amongst those who remember the former temple.

Introduction

Now the building work proper begins. The next short section is joined to the previous one by the conjunction 'then.' In other words, work on the temple project cannot start until the altar and the appropriate sacrifices have been offered. Once that point is firmly established (as v. 6 clearly does) then our attention switches to the temple work.

The passage is relatively straightforward and contains – as we shall see – many echoes of the first temple construction. The reader is supposed to see a continuity between that first temple and this second one. For sure, the exile has taken place in between, the Persians still have power over the land and there is no king from David's line ruling on the throne but in many other ways it is business as usual. This is an important point for understanding the enigmatic verse 12 where there is both joy and weeping amongst those who remember the last temple.

There are one or two issues to wrestle with within the text, not least how the passage can be harmonised with two other related portions of Scripture:

- In 3:8 Zerubbabel appears to be taking the lead in the building work yet Ezra 5:16 identifies Sheshbazzar rather than Zerubbabel as the one who commenced the building project. But these

two verses need not be mutually incompatible.
We know that Cyrus appointed Sheshbazzar as
the official governor (5:14) which may be why
he is noted in 1:11 as being the one who received
the returned items from the temple. However,
it is quite possible that Zerubbabel bore prime
responsibility for the work whilst Sheshbazzar,
in his capacity as official governor, laid the
ceremonial stone.

- In Ezra 3 the temple's foundation is laid.
  However, in Haggai 2 which describes events
  twelve years later, we also read a reference to the
  temple's foundation being laid (Hag. 2:15-18).
  Again, this need not be the contradiction it
  might appear. In Haggai 2 the people are being
  called to return to the rebuilding of the temple,
  a task that had never been finished. Haggai calls
  on them to 'give careful thought to the day when
  the foundation of the Lord's temple was laid' but
  he does not specify when that day was. It is quite
  possible that Haggai is simply calling on the
  people to recall the beginning of the rebuilding
  with all its fervent commitment, as recorded
  back in Ezra 3.

Returning to our passage in Ezra, key to understanding
Ezra 3:7-13 is verse 12: 'But many of the older priests
and Levites and family heads, who had seen the former
temple, wept aloud when they saw the foundations of
this temple being laid, while many others shouted for joy.'
Understanding this perplexing verse is key to drawing
clear and sharp applications from the text.

Listening to the text

Context and structure

The text falls neatly into two:

- The building work (3:7-9)

- The people's response (3:10-13)

Working through the text

The building work (3:7-9)

The original hearers of this section would have recognised many echoes of the way the first temple was constructed. The author wants them to see the continuity between that temple and this one. The building material once again is cedar logs and it comes from the same source, Lebanon (compare 2 Chron. 2:3 with Ezra 3:7); work begins in the same month (compare 2 Chron. 3:2 with Ezra 3:8);[6] the people even – as we shall see – sing the same song (compare 2 Chron. 5:13 with Ezra 3:11).[7] The work on the temple was a highly important and honourable task and we should see that reflected in the careful record in 3:9 of the names of those who supervised this work. Indeed, it is best to see these names as continuing the list we first encountered in chapter

---

6. Some commentators point out that this was the dry month and therefore a suitable time to begin work, but this rather cold approach to the text ignores the significance that attaches to dates (e.g. Ezra 3:1 and the festival celebrations).

7. There are a number of precise textual issues arising in the list of names in v. 9, in particular how many different groups there are and how Hebrew names should be translated (compare NIV 'Hodaviah' with ESV 'Judah'). A technical commentary will explain some of these differences but the main point remains: the temple work is started with everyone playing their part.

2. The 'they' of 3:7 who gave money and provisions to get the work underway are almost certainly a continuation of the 'one man' theme from 3:1. Here is a project overseen by a chosen few but in which everybody participates.

There are some details about this building work which are different from the building of the first temple, but these are minor and probably pragmatic. For example, the Levites who supervised the rebuilding had to be over twenty (3:8) whereas those who supervised the building of the first temple had to be over thirty (1 Chron. 23:3-4). The drop in the age restriction was probably just to increase the number of Levites who were eligible to help, given that there were now far fewer of them overall (only seventy-four Levites are recorded as returning in Ezra 2:4 whereas there are 24,000 Levites recorded in 1 Chron.).

The people's response (3:10-13)

The second part of the passage details the people's response. Again, there are strong echoes of Solomon's building project: the assembly of the priests (2 Chron. 5:11); the musicians with their trumpets and cymbals (2 Chron. 5:12); and of course the explicit references in the text back to the Davidic plans (v. 10) and David's song (v. 11).

This covenant song is sung by all the people. The 'they' of verse 11 (those who sang) are the 'they' of verse 7 (those who gave) and also the 'they' of verse 1 (those who assembled together as one). This covenant unity is also echoed in the shout of praise that is offered up by all the people (v. 11b). The words of the song are almost exactly the same as those offered up in Solomon's day: 'He is good, his love endures for ever' (2 Chron. 5:13), the only minor difference being the addition of the phrase 'to Israel.' Such an addition would not have been needed in the heady days of King Solomon when Israel was the powerhouse nation. Now, however, things have changed. Blessing seems to have fallen on other nations – not least Babylon and Persia. The addition of the word 'Israel' is necessary therefore to demonstrate the particular focus of the Lord's affection in these more multi-national times.

There is though one major difference from the events of Solomon's day which would not have escaped those who knew their Scriptures well. The first shout of thanks in the days of Solomon was offered not at the *start* of building work but at its *end* (2 Chron. 5). The chapter in Chronicles describes the completion of the building work and – as such – is more closely paralleled with Ezra 6, not Ezra 3. 2 Chronicles 3-5 is full of completion terminology (for example, 'When all the work Solomon had done for the temple of the Lord was finished…' 2 Chron. 5:1). Things are different in Ezra's day. The people's shout of praise occurs only at the laying of the foundation stone (v. 10). The author of Ezra would have known the Chronicles account and so presumably wants to highlight that the timing here is different We will find some useful points of application in this contrast (see below).

The celebrations continue, again emphasising the people's joy at this foundation stage (v. 11). The temple is not yet built, not even remotely so, and yet great praise pours forth from the people of God as they see the Lord beginning to fulfil His promises.

However, joy is not the only emotion. Verses 12 and 13 tell us that some felt the opposite emotion, sadness. This weeping aloud is limited to the older returning exiles who – we are specifically told – 'had seen the former temple'

– a clear clue to the nature of the sadness. This sadness was mixed together with the joyful shouts so that 'no one could distinguish the sound of the shouts of joy from the sound of weeping.'[8]

The key question then becomes why were these older people weeping? There are a number of possibilities. The most common suggestion is that this new temple simply isn't the size of the old one. After all, that would explain the reference to having 'seen the former temple.' In other words, when these old men saw the foundations they recognised from the footprint of the new structure that the new temple would be less glorious than the first one in terms of its size. However, this view is unwarranted. We read of the former temple's dimensions in 1 Kings 6:2. It is 27m long, 9m wide and 14m high (NIV footnote, translating 'cubits' into metric units). We also know about some of the dimensions of the new temple: 'it is to be [27m] high and [27m] wide' according to Cyrus' original decree (Ezra 6:3). Even though one dimension of the new temple is missing from this account, the general picture is that, if anything, the new temple is actually likely to be *larger* than the old one. So, physical size seems very unlikely to be the issue here.

---

8. Some commentators strangely want to make these tears of joy (like those shed by an Olympic athlete on the medal podium). But this will not do: the text paints the response as one of contrast to the joy both in the 'but' that introduces v. 12 and the conflicting emotions presented in v. 13. Alternatively, Fyall sees the tears as 'the beginning of the spirit of defeatism which is to be condemned by Haggai and is to be a continuing problem as the work progresses.' However, that seems to me to be reading far too much negativity into the otherwise overwhelmingly positive text. Fyall, R., *The message of Ezra & Haggai* (Nottingham, UK: Inter-Varsity Press, 2010), p. 69.

A second contender as an explanation of the weeping is that the rebuilt temple lacked the splendour of old one in terms of its architecture and furnishings. But this too seems unlikely. There is no doubt that Solomon's temple was a sumptuous affair. But at this point, these older men were only looking at foundations. The building work was yet to get going. There was plenty of money for the rebuilding and the plundered treasures from the old temple were now returned, ready to be placed in the new one. So it is hard to see how at this point there could be any assessment of exactly how lavish the final structure and interior of the temple might be.

A third suggestion is that this sadness is caused by re-membering the sin and national apostasy that had brought them to this moment. Again, this seems an unlikely explanation as there is no reason why any such sadness should be confined to those who had seen the previous temple. The national consciousness of sin seems to have been universal: that was the point made in 3:1-6.

Probably the best explanation of this sadness is concerned not with size or lavishness or apostasy but with the Lord's glory. The supreme glory of the first temple was not its size or lavish furnishings but that the presence of the Lord was there. This presence of the Lord was intimately connected with the presence of the Ark of the Covenant in the Holy of Holies. The glory of the Lord descended on the first temple as the Ark was placed for the first time in the Holy of Holies (2 Chron. 5). But there will be no Ark in this new temple. The glory of the presence of the Lord will never fill this temple in that way. After all the continuity motifs in this chapter, here is a great discontinuity with the former temple.

In the first temple consecration the covenant song was sung and the glory descended on to the Ark in the Holy of Holies. Now in this second temple consecration the same covenant song is sung and nothing happens – nothing *can* happen – because the Ark is absent. This seems to be the most likely explanation of the sadness of those who knew the former temple. The glory of the Lord will be absent from this new temple because the Ark will be absent from it. As we read on, we find that this is indeed the case. When the new temple is finally complete (Ezra 6:14), the descending cloud is noticeable by its absence (particularly because this had also characterised the tabernacle completion in Exod. 40:34).

There are two main objections to this solution.[9] The first (and more powerful one) is that it is an argument from silence and we should be wary of building too much upon such logic. We are right to be cautious about arguments from silence. But they should not be dismissed out of hand. Moreover, this is not an argument from silence when we look at the wider Biblical context and draw in truths from other Scriptures. The text in Ezra clearly encourages us to ask the question, 'Why were they weeping?' and the text *seen in its whole Biblical context* also, I believe, answers the question.

That brings us to the second objection which is related to the first. This objection is based on the argument that every Bible book must be able to be understood on its own, apart from the rest of Scripture. The argument is that the original readers would only have had this text and

9. A solution which is not novel to me, by the way. It is picked up, in some measure, in Verhoef, P., *The books of Haggai and Malachi*, New International Commentary on the Old Testament (Grand Rapids, USA: Eerdmans, 1987), p. 97.

so we must find all our answers here in Ezra or not at all. But such an objection is a perversion of the doctrine of Scripture. The Spirit has inspired and preserved the whole canon to be read and understood together. There are, for example, a number of indications in Ezra that the author expected his readers to know the Chronicles account of the first temple.

In summary, there was clearly something about the second temple which provoked sadness in those who remembered the first. I think that the best explanation of this is the absence of the Ark and the absence of the glorious presence of Yahweh which the Ark was seen to confer.

There is one extra piece of the jigsaw to consider, however. Ezra's account of the beginning of the new temple must surely draw us to reflect on Ezekiel's prophecy about the post-exilic temple (Ezek. 40-48). Ezekiel's message from the Lord was spoken to the people of Israel in exile to show them the reason for their spiritual adultery and also to give them hope for the future. That hope, most clearly expressed in Ezekiel's latter chapters, includes the promise of a glorious new temple. This is not just Solomon's temple restored, the temple Ezekiel describes is out-of-this-world in terms of both size and glory.

How does this connect with Ezra 3 and the tears of those who remembered the former temple? It is quite possible that those who had not known *any* temple saw Ezekiel 40 being fulfilled in Zerubbabel and Joshua's building project and so were full of joy. On one level, the level of immediate fulfilment, they were right. Ezekiel's temple sounded very other-worldly but prophets did use exalted language at times to describe heady events of great theological significance.

However, those who remembered the first temple might have realised that the Ezra construction was simply more of the same – it was another temple which, like the first temple, would fall short of being the full and final fulfilment of Ezekiel's prophecies. There must be something more. It may be that the tears that day were prompted not just by comparisons with the old temple but by comparisons with the temple Ezekiel had promised too. Something more was needed; something more was to come.

From text to message

The main points of application come from seeing the temple construction in Ezra 3 in the context of temple building and prophecy in the whole Bible. It is important to find ways to do this which engage our hearers and allow the text to drive the message and the applications.

Getting the message clear: the theme

The second temple is started and brings forth joy and sadness.

Getting the message clear: the aim

There is a 'now' and 'not yet' about the construction work of Ezra 3. It is the fulfilment of all that God has promised and yet it is not going to deliver the glory days that some remember or hope for. We find the same tension when we come to Christ, the true temple. There is great glory in the New Covenant now but we must be reminded that it is nothing compared to what is to come when Christ is finally revealed.

A way in

The text makes clear that this response of the people is a response to the foundation of the temple being laid (v. 10, repeated v. 11). The people are responding to the beginning of the building project, not its completion. A way in which runs with the grain of the text will introduce this concept. For example, imagine walking past a building site where work has just got started. There is nothing very impressive about a hole in the ground. Stone (if there is any) is not dressed and ready to use. Wood is not planed and finished. It all looks a bit rough and ready and it's difficult to imagine what the final building will look like. However, it is precisely this kind of building site which makes the Israelites dress up and celebrate – most of them anyway.

An alternative approach would be to take some of the application ideas and lead in with those. For example, many Christians are just too positive! There need to be a few tears as well sometimes if we are to be in tune with what God is doing and has promised to do *and what He has not done yet*. Conversely, many Christians (probably the majority) are too negative. There are too many tears: there needs to be some joy in even the smallest things God is doing amongst us.

Ideas for application

- God is keeping His promise to restore the temple. However, this temple is not the glorious one promised; something more is needed and has been promised. One day Christ, the true temple, will come.

- As we look at the earthly ministry of Christ there is glory, especially in the cross and resurrection.

But we do not yet see Christ as He is now, in the fullness of His glory. That moment is still to come. Christians need to feel this tension.

- As regards our walk with Christ too, there needs to be both joy and sadness: joy in what we are now in Christ, joy in what He has done and is doing but also sadness in what we are not yet. Alongside this sadness though there should be an expectation that one day sin and sadness will disappear and there will be only joy.

- This joy and sadness needs to apply to the work of building the church community also. There is joy even in the foundation work. Christians need to cultivate a sense of joy in every building opportunity: every gospel moment, every teenager at a youth group (however draining and rowdy), every brief conversation with a neighbour, every small battle with sin won. These are 'holes in the ground' but we need to learn to find joy in them. However, we also need to have appropriate sadness: this is not it. We can find too much glory in this world, forgetting that the full glory days are yet to come. Our sadness should reflect a sense of longing. The church of Christ is not as it should be now but one day all our expectations will be fulfilled.

Suggestions for preaching

Sermon 1
A sermon on this passage needs to capture the tension that the text contains.

- **Covenant continuity.** The strong sense of continuity between Ezra 3 and the building of the first temple reminds us of God's continuing faithfulness to the covenants He made with His people under Moses and David. The temple had a key place in both these covenants and in His sovereignty God has brought the exiles back to rebuild it. Remembering that God keeps His covenants points us forward too. There are covenant words which have yet to be fulfilled. The physical temple building looks forward to a spiritual house – Christ Himself, with us being built up into Him (1 Pet. 2:4-8). This is where the theme of covenant continuity will lead.

- **Covenant rejoicing.** The continuity brings forth rejoicing. The same song is repeated from the first temple project but noticeably it now comes at the start of the building work, not its completion. Such is the anticipation of the Israelites that even the holes in the ground that represent the temple foundations are a cause for rejoicing. We need to learn to cultivate the same sense of joy at everything God is doing for us and through us in Christ Jesus.

- **Covenant weeping.** Yet there is an uneasiness about the Israelites. Some of the older, wiser men remember the past and realise that this glory moment is not *the* glory moment. It cannot be. There is something greater to come. We live this side of the incarnation when the true temple has come and lived among us and given Himself yet still we need to feel this tension: these may be glorious days (and we should pray they are) but they are not *the* glory days.

Sermon 2

It would be possible to group the two parts of chapter 3 together although as I explained in the previous chapter, the first part of chapter 3 perhaps belongs better with the latter part of chapter 2. Nevertheless, a sermon taking the whole of chapter 3 together could expand on the outline I suggested in Sermon 1, even though some points would have to be dropped:

- Covenant relationship: first things first (v. 1-3)
- Covenant obedience: keeping the Law (v. 4-6)
- Covenant rejoicing: building the temple (v. 7-11)
- Covenant weeping: more to come? (v. 12-13)

Suggestions for teaching

Questions to help understand the passage

1. Scan 2 Chronicles 3-5. What similarities do you notice between the first and second building projects? Are there any differences? If so, what?

2. When did the covenant song get sung first time around (see 2 Chron. 5:13)? When does it get sung this time (v. 10, v. 11)?

3. Why are the people rejoicing (v. 11)?

4. What might some of the reasons be for the weeping (v. 12-13)? Try to evaluate some of these biblically. You might like to use 2 Chronicles 5:13-14; Ezra 6:3 (compare 1 Kings 6:2) and Ezekiel 40.

5. What is missing in this account (use Jer. 3:14-18 as a prompt)?

Questions to help apply the passage

1. Remind yourself about the significance of the temple as it points us towards Christ (see John 2:20-21) and the church (see 1 Pet. 2:4-8).

2. What are the foundations we see today in our personal and church life?

3. How can we cultivate a sense of joy over even these small beginnings?

4. What reasons are there for Christians to weep?

5. How do we train ourselves to find both joy and godly sorrow in the here and now?

6. What do Christians have to look forward to? Look at Ezekiel 48:35 for a prompt.

5. Surrounded by enemies
(Ezra 4:1-5)

Enemies ask the Jewish leaders if they can help with rebuilding the temple. The leaders refuse. The local people then
try to stop the Jewish people continuing with the rebuilding
and bribe officials to work against them. This opposition
continued all through Cyrus' reign and into Darius'.

Introduction

The first five verses of Chapter 4 describe the external
opposition to the rebuilding of the temple which led to the
work stopping for over a decade. This standstill in the work
is described in the last verse of chapter 4, 'Thus the work
on the house of God in Jerusalem came to a standstill until
the second year of the reign of Darius king of Persia' (4:24).

What will seem strange though to twenty-first-century
readers is that in between these first five verses about the
current opposition to *temple* rebuilding and the last verse,
v. 24 about the effect of this current opposition, the author
has inserted a long section describing external opposition
to *city wall* rebuilding from a much later time.

This middle section of chapter 4 (4:6-23) describes
external opposition to the building of the city walls which
took place in the much later reigns of Xerxes (4:6) and
Artaxerxes (4:7-23). We need to ask what the author is
trying to do in putting his material together in this way.

It seems most likely that he is trying to present to us a
complete picture of the external opposition to the various
rebuilding works and so he groups all the occurrences of
this together. This way of grouping material by theme

rather than precise chronology was not unusual for ancient writers nor was it seen as problematic.

The author chooses to spend most time on the story from the reign of King Artaxerxes. This may be because it was the best documented (as it mainly consisted of an interchange of official correspondence). More probably, it may simply best do the job that the inspired author wants done, that is, to represent the variety and entirety of the types and methods of opposition. If this is the case, it works very well!

It is not therefore playing fast and loose with history to bring all this material together with the conclusion, 'thus the work on the house of God in Jerusalem came to a standstill until the second year of the reign of Darius king of Persia'. Rather, it is saying, in effect, 'it is precisely *this* kind of opposition that caused the temple rebuilding to stop.'

The Bible study leader or preacher will need to make some judgments about how much of this background and chronology to share with a group or congregation. Some Christians may be confused with this mixing of timelines; others, frankly, may not notice. It will vary from one setting to another. Either way, the preacher or teacher must do enough to make sure that questions people have about chronology do not detract from the point the author is trying to make.

All this said, the chapter *does* follow a linear timeline even though it is a compressed one. The conclusion of verse 24 that the rebuilding of the temple stopped flows out of the author's presentation in the whole chapter of how God's work is always opposed.

- Verses 1-3 Opposition against the leaders. This seems to occur early on in the building process, in the reign of Cyrus (539 B.C.–530 B.C.).

- Verses 4-5 Opposition against the people. This follows on from verse 1-3 but describes more generally the period down to the beginning of the reign of Darius (say, 539 B.C.–522 B.C.).

- Verse 6 is a very brief summary of the opposition during the reign of Xerxes (also known as Ahasuerus). (He reigned from 486 B.C.–464 B.C.).

- Verses 7-23 focus on two particular oppositions which took place in the reign of Artaxerxes.[10] One is described very briefly (a letter from four troublemakers and their associates). The second opposition takes up the majority of the passage; it contains first the accusation from Rehum and Shimshai (vv. 9-16) and then the king's reply (vv. 17-22).

Listening to the text

Context and structure

Chapter 4 is a long unit made up of different opposition stories. It is quite possible to preach it as one: indeed, such an approach might reflect its primary purpose in the stories being grouped together in this way. I will suggest a way of doing this in the next chapter. However I have also divided the material in Chapter 4 into two sections,

---

10. It is possible that this describes one letter, not two. However, the two sets of different names seem to make this unlikely. It makes little difference to how the passage is taught or preached.

focusing on the first here. There are a couple of reasons for suggesting this division:

First, there is probably too much material in Chapter 4 to do justice to it all in a single sermon. This is particularly so if some explanation of how the passage functions is required. If you are not aiming to include this, then a single sermon or study becomes more feasible.

More importantly, the two kinds of opposition are quite different. In verses 1-5 the opposition is direct and personal, being directed at either the leaders or the people themselves. In verses 6-23 the opposition is impersonal, as official letters pass to and fro. In fact, the people of God may have known nothing about it!

Focusing just on 4:1-5, this shorter passage splits neatly into two:

- Opposition against leaders (4:1-3)

- Opposition against the people (4:4-5)

Finally, it is worth observing how this chapter about opposition functions within Ezra. The opposition is clearly portrayed as being successful. The work of rebuilding stops. There is little encouragement in this chapter of the sort which says, 'If you do this or that you will avoid these problems.' That will come in Ezra 5. For the moment, though, this section serves as a sobering reality check. It shows the hearer the nature and effect of opposition to God's work, opposition which appears, for a while at least, to be effective. We should let this drive our application. It is no use the preacher softening the blow and shock by saying, 'Thankfully, we know we can't be defeated.' Like other warning passages in the Bible, Ezra 4 does not give us a guilt-free 'happy ever after', instead it wakes us up to danger. Its message is like Peter's warning: 'Be alert and sober-minded. Your enemy the devil prowls around like a roaring lion looking for someone to devour' (1 Pet. 5:8). Ezra 4 serves, as much as anything, to help us hear him roar.

Working through the text

Opposition against leaders (4:1-3)

The first conflict is between some surrounding peoples and Zerubbabel, Joshua and the heads of the families. These opponents may be the same peoples we've already met in 3:3. But who are they? They appear to have a semblance of orthodoxy about them – after all, they introduce themselves by saying to the Jewish leaders, 'we seek your God and have been sacrificing to him since the time of Esarhaddon, king of Assyria, who brought us here' (v. 2).

No doubt the offer of help was welcome in terms of manpower as well as sounding rather genuine. We've already seen that just seventy-four Levites (at most) were available to supervise the work compared to the 24,000 employed on Solomon's temple. Every little helps! But the text allows us no such sentimentality. Both directly and indirectly we are able to see through this offer just as Zerubbabel, Joshua and the other leaders do.

In terms of direct evidence, verse 1 introduces the people offering to help in strongly negative terms, calling them 'the enemies of Judah and Benjamin.' This is the first time this tribal pairing of Judah and Benjamin has appeared since 1:5 where it was used to indicate those whose hearts God had moved. So for 'enemies of Judah and Benjamin' we should probably read 'those whose hearts God had *not* moved.'

There are various strands of indirect evidence too which point the reader to the true nature of those offering to help. First, these people are rather loose in the way they describe their worship. 'We seek your God and have been sacrificing to him.' (4:2). Notice both the pronoun 'your' and the absence of the divine name. Zerubbabel certainly seems to pick up on these tell-tale signs and replies and corrects their theological grammar, 'We alone will build it for the LORD, the God of Israel.'

Second, the history of these enemies gives them away. As we noted in the introduction these are the people the Assyrians resettled. King Esarhaddon of Assyria (the successor to Sennacherib, see 2 Kings 19:37) resettled much of his father's conquered territory after the attack on Jerusalem, including most of the southern kingdom of Judah. As we saw before, the Assyrian strategy was to recolonize captured lands with a mix of peoples and therefore a mix of religions too. There was no pure Yahweh worship established in Judah. Any worship of Israel's God was mixed in with other cults. 'They worshipped the LORD, but they also served their own gods in accordance with the customs of the nations from which they had been brought' (2 Kings 17:33). So whilst it might have been true that the people in Ezra 4:2 had been sacrificing to Israel's God, this would have been far from the whole story.[11]

Third, genuine Yahweh-worshippers would have been happy for the building work to be carried out whether or not they were involved. Only enemies of the Lord would begrudge what others did for him. Quite what these enemies hoped to

---

11. Interestingly, many Biblical historians see here the beginnings of the Jewish-Samaritan divide that so clearly existed at the time of the Gospels.

achieve by 'helping out' is not made clear nor are we invited to speculate. It is enough to know that these people were enemies of the work and therefore of the God who ordained it.

Zerubbabel, Joshua and the other leaders answer clearly and directly. They make clear that these enemies can have no part in building the temple of 'the LORD, the God of Israel'. However, it is important to note that their response is also wise. This wisdom is seen in the fact that the Jewish leaders add that they have been commissioned to build this temple by King Cyrus. This is not panic on their part. Rather, it is a demonstration of wisdom to ensure that there can be no comeback. Such a response is not indicative of a lack of faith, as some would have. No, it is a prime example of being 'shrewd as snakes and as innocent as doves' (Matt. 10:16).

Opposition against the people (4:4-5)

Now the focus switches. In verses 4-5 it is the Jewish people rather than their leaders who are the target of the opposition. There is no indication that this new opposition comes from a different group of enemies. It seems we are still reading about those identified as enemies in verse 1 though now they are simply called 'the people around them' (v. 4). However, their target is now the Jewish people themselves and their objectives are spelt out more clearly. These opponents want to 'discourage' the people of Israel and 'make them afraid to go on building.' The word 'discouraged' (NIV, ESV) is a succinct translation of a phrase which literally means 'weaken the hands.' How did this discouragement take place? The next verse probably provides the answer. 'They bribed officials to work against them and frustrate their plans.' This verse may give an insight into why the author writes next about later opposition in the days of Artaxerxes. This next section is all about opposition to God's work from officials. It may be that it is included next to give an example of precisely the kind of trouble that officials can stir up.

What is clear is that the opposition described in Ezra 4:4-5 worked: the building work came to a halt (4:24).

From text to message

This is a sobering passage and preachers must not soften the blow of its hard message. The overriding message is that opposition works. For sure, the story gets resolved but for now we must let the tone and sobriety of the passage do its work.

Getting the message clear: the theme

Opposition can be subtle, can target specific groups and can work.

Getting the message clear: the aim

Learn to spot opposition; expect it and know how our enemy, the devil, prowls around. It won't surprise sermon hearers or Bible study members to see the link between Israel and Jesus. The devil is implacably opposed to all of God's work but his opposition is seen most clearly in the way he opposed the Son of God, following many of the same strategies he used in Ezra 4. Those who follow Christ should expect nothing less.

A way in

This is not a laugh-a-minute topic and I believe hearers need a sober introduction to get them thinking clearly. It is possible to paint a (hopefully theoretical) picture about the damage Satan wants to do to those who are in Christ and to Christ's church. The devil hates Christ's work, His temple (the church) and His glory and will do all he can to derail them. But he is nothing if not predictable. He may be a powerful enemy, prowling around like a lion, but his devouring strategy is obvious when we know what we are looking for.

Alternatively, I have used an introduction based on hymnology – making the point that no one seems to write songs about fighting these days. We march *against* war, we don't sing about it. A former enthusiasm amongst evangelicals for military language and music has dwindled and that's a worrying trend, for the Bible leaves us in no doubt that we are in a battle. And key to winning a battle is enemy intelligence: knowing where the enemy is and how he means to attack. That is the inside information that Ezra 4 gives us.

Ideas for application

- We need to see that opposition is real and dangerous. Satan is against Yahweh and His plans.

- Opposition can sometimes seem very credible. Many are seduced by fine-sounding words from those who claim they worship the same God. There are warnings here for those tempted by multi-faith projects and some ecumenical approaches too. However I do not see the message of this chapter as necessarily being a warning against what we call co-belligerence (for example, working together with those of other faiths over issues like abortion) so the preacher or leader must be careful not to over-apply the warning contained in this passage. The key to avoiding such mistakes is to realise that it is the temple-building project that is at the heart of the kingdom work, which, in today's terms, is the gospel work of building Christ's church. It is *this* work that we cannot and must not share with those who do not belong to Christ.

- The opposition attacks leaders first and we should not be surprised at this priority. If Zerubbabel and Joshua cave in, the job is done and all the bribes (v. 4) are saved. This means that a key application is to appoint wise leaders in the church and see they are properly supported, especially in prayer, so that they will both be discerning and stand firm.

- We need to notice that once leaders stand firm, the attacks continue elsewhere. It is a less efficient strategy for Satan to attack churches by undermining members, as opposed to leaders, but it is no less effective when successful, as verses 4-5 show. All believers need therefore to be vigilant against such attacks.

- Satan employed the same strategy of attacking the leader first when confronting Christ. Satan first attacked Jesus both physically (Matt. 2:13-18) and then more directly spiritually (Matt. 4:1-11). Both attacks were repulsed. Success in either would have meant the end of God's plan. Satan's strategy then switched to people around Jesus (Peter, Matt. 16:23 and more significantly, Judas, Matt. 26:14-16). It appeared to be a strategy that worked, leading to the death of the Son and the desertion of His disciples, though we know all this was part of a bigger plan and not the end of the story.

Suggestions for preaching

Sermon 1

Christians must think soberly about Satan and his opposition: this chapter helps us to see clearly how and where the devil works so that we can spot his attacks. In the light of the whole of Scripture, it cannot be wrong to see the hand of Satan behind the events of Ezra. It is also good to show congregations that Satan often attacks through people or circumstances. I think it is helpful to point out that this kind of opposition is exactly the kind of opposition Christ Himself faced. This will keep us from making a direct line from 'them then' to 'us now', something which is not always helpful or appropriate.

- **The enemy's attack starts with leaders.** Here, the preacher needs to show the priority of the enemy's strategy. It is clearly more efficient to attack and bring down leaders. Such attacks can be very subtle (as this one is) and we need leaders of the calibre of Zerubbabel and Joshua to see through the fog and stand firm. This means the church needs to exercise care in appointing leaders and wisdom in supporting them – especially spiritually. Many churches take good leaders for granted. We need those who are 'shrewd as snakes and innocent as doves.'

- **The enemy's attack comes to us all.** If leaders stand firm, Satan attacks the 'people'. This is

a less efficient strategy but no less effective if
not withstood. Here, the focus shifts and the
people are worn down through discouragement.
Soberingly, this strategy works and the halt of
verse 24 kicks in. Temple-building work stops
for up to fifteen or sixteen years. Little is done
to further the kingdom work. We need therefore
to keep standing firm together. We need to
watch out for one another and have a spirit in
our churches which allows challenge, prayer,
honesty and integrity when it comes to tacking
sin. Otherwise, our gospel work will also grind
to a halt.

The preacher will have to decide where to leave this sermon. Personally, when preaching a series I am quite content to leave an individual sermon on a sobering note,
perhaps with just a very small glimmer of hope to come in
a future message. We need to feel the pain of this chapter
and providing a 'Happy Ever After' ending to every sermon
may lead to complacency.

Sermon 2
I will consider a sermon which tackles the whole of 4:1-24
in the next chapter.

Suggestions for teaching
Questions to help understand the passage

1. What clues are there in the passage that these people
    are indeed 'enemies' (v. 1)? Check out 2 Kings 17:33
    for some help.

2. Why do you suppose these enemies go first to the leaders?

3. How do the leaders respond?

4. Where now do the enemies turn?

5. How are the people attacked and how do they respond?

6. What is the end result (4:24)?

Questions to help apply the passage

1. What parallels do you see here with the life of Christ and the opposition He faced?

2. What is the spiritual reality behind Ezra 4 and all opposition to God's work?

3. How do we help leaders stand firm? Be practical and commit to some actions.

4. How do we help one another stand firm? What kind of atmosphere does there need to be in church in order to facilitate this mutual help and encouragement? Think of practical things you could do.

5. How will the whole story end, do you think?

6. Opposition works…(Ezra 4:6-24)

Later, in the reign of King Xerxes, officials accuse the Jews (4:6). Later still, in the reign of King Artaxerxes, other officials write two letters to the king. The second letter and its effects are recorded in detail. Here, officials warn the king that letting the Jews rebuild Jerusalem will bankrupt him. The king writes back, agreeing. As a result the Jews are forced to stop rebuilding the city (4:7-23). These additional examples of opposition serve to help explain why the earlier work on the temple stopped (4:24).

Introduction

As we have already seen, the action in this section jumps chronologically to the reign of Xerxes (4:6, 486 B.C.) and then on into the reign of Artaxerxes (4:7, his reign commenced in 464 B.C.). However, these events are grouped together here with earlier opposition stories (4:1-5) to show the continuous and comprehensive nature of the opposition God's people faced – first as they sought to rebuild the temple (4:1) and then in this section as they seek to rebuild the walls (4:12). We should not imagine there was ever any let up.

Most focus is given to the details of what happened in the reign of Artaxerxes (vv. 7-23). Although all these events take place long after the temple is completed, the narrator has brought them forward and represented them as being part of his explanation of why work on the temple halted (v. 24). We should not be alarmed at the way the text here moves back and forth between different times in history. The author simply wants to use the best story to illustrate the nature and depths of the opposition that will always work against God and His people.

Like the first part of chapter 4, the story here is bleak. The opposition is successful and does the job for which it was intended. As such, we have to assume the section functions in two ways. First, it is to show us that opposition is real and effective. Second, the detail we are given functions to show us how opposition works, presumably so that we can be ready to spot it.

The action in this section takes place in the reigns of two later kings of Persia. Xerxes, the first king mentioned (4:6), spent a great deal of money on wars and so his son, Artaxerxes (4:7), inherited an almost bankrupt kingdom. It is not surprising therefore that Israel's enemies play on Artaxerxes' financial insecurity by suggesting that a rebuilt Jerusalem would threaten his finances (4:13). The two kings mentioned here appear elsewhere in the Bible too. Xerxes is the king who married Esther. Artaxerxes employed Nehemiah as his cup-bearer and allowed him to return to Jerusalem to rebuild the city walls (Neh. 2:1f).

It is most likely that the opposition to rebuilding Jerusalem described in Ezra 4 is not the same opposition that we read about in Nehemiah. Certainly, the names of the opponents are different.

Something else to note about this section is that it contains the beginning of one of the two sections of the book written in Aramaic, the official written language of the Persian Empire (4:9-6:18 and 7:12-26).[12] The primary significance of that to this part of chapter 4 is that it lends extra weight to the authenticity of the account. This account contains the contents of two official letters and the original

---

12. The only other Aramaic section in the Old Testament is found in Daniel 2:4-7:28.

letters would have been written in Aramaic. If the author of Ezra were copying these letters from the official archive it would be natural for him to use their original language. The use of Aramaic here is not confined to these letters but this is probably less significant than we might imagine. There was a *lingua franca*, a common language, spoken across the Persian Empire, and Aramaic was this language in written form. So it is very likely that the author of Ezra would have been comfortable in both Hebrew and Aramaic and able to switch easily between the two. Possibly the author began using Aramaic when copying the first official document and then just continued in that language until he reached a particularly significant moment in the story. The place the author stops using Aramaic (Ezra 6:18) may be of more significance theologically as we shall see when we arrive there.

Listening to the text
Context and structure
The second part of chapter 4 has a simple structure and continues on the opposition theme we encountered in the first section of chapter 4:

- Two brief opposition stories (4:6-7)
- An opposition letter (4:8-16)
- The king's reply (4:17-22)
- Conclusion (4:23-24)

Working through the text
Two brief opposition stories (4:6-7)
The first incident is an accusation against the Jews made in Xerxes' reign (4:6). The 'they', who made this accusation seems to refer back to 'the peoples around them' (4:4), that

is, the other people who lived in Jerusalem. It seems that the locals made trouble for the Jews in every era.

The second incident is a letter written to the next king, Artaxerxes, by a list of named individuals (4:7). The reference to language in 4:7 prepares us for the account that will follow (although the Aramaic section does not actually begin until verse 9).

The author of Ezra chooses to omit many of the details of these two incidents. He does not record the names of the accusers in the first incident or details of the contents of either letter. This is in sharp contrast to the long and detailed account of the last accusation (4:8-23). This difference in form is probably best explained by a difference in purpose. The more detailed account is meant to give us insights into how opposition *works*. The earlier, briefer stories are there to show us that opposition *exists* and that it *continues* throughout the reigns of all the kings of Persia. There is, in other words, no let up.

Moreover, the accounts in verses 6-7 lend weight to the rather sweeping statement of verse 5, where the author claims that the peoples around the Jews, 'bribed officials to work against them and frustrate their plans during the entire reign of Cyrus, king of Persia and down to the reign of Darius king of Persia'. This might sound like hyperbole. But by recording incidents of opposition from the two kings who followed Darius, the author is confirming that opposition really was never-ending.

An opposition letter (4:8-16)

First, we are introduced to the two main objectors and their roles. Rehum is called 'the commanding officer' and Shimshai 'the secretary'. The exact nature of these job titles is not specified though Rehum is clearly a man with authority. The fact that Shimshai is included in the account probably means that being 'the secretary' was a fairly senior post also. We should perhaps think more in terms of the UK civil service nomenclature where 'secretary' indicates a senior leadership role.[13] Also, an Aramaic translation of this term is used to refer to Ezra (7:21) and Ezra's role is more than that of lowly office clerk. What is clear is that these two officials are at least locally significant, a fact confirmed by the manner in which their correspondence prompts a personal and prompt reply from the King.

The motives of these men are made clear as soon as they are introduced. We are told in 4:8 that these two men are 'against Jerusalem'. Once again this is an opposition story writ large.

The preamble to the letter (vv. 9-10) is extraordinary. Clearly Rehum and Shimshai are the movers and shakers but they claim the support of virtually the entire known world. The letter provides an insight into the kind of opposition strategies that will be employed against God's people and here is the first strategy: a tendency in God's enemies to exaggerate those they claim to represent.

The 'rest of their associates' presumably includes all the public officials: 'the judges and officials.' But look at the area they are from! Although we are uncertain about 'Tripolis' (most likely an area but it could also be a class of officialdom) the clearly geographic descriptions are comprehensive. 'Persia, Erech and Babylon, the Elamites of Susa, and the other people...settled in the city of Samaria

---

13. Either in the ministers of the crown who are called Secretary of State for, say, Education, or in the civil servants who work in their ministries who have such titles as Permanent Secretary and Under-Secretary.

and elsewhere in Trans-Euphrates' describes – in essence – the entire centre section of mighty Persian empire. Only outlying posts (e.g. India and Cush, see Esther 1:1) are omitted. The description includes the ancient capital of the empire, Babylon, and its spring capital, Susa.

The phrase 'Trans-Euphrates' is worthy of closer examination because it will recur in verses 16, 17 and 20. It is almost certainly an official description of an area, probably the huge area west of the Euphrates river up to the Mediterranean, an area that would have included Jerusalem. Even a cursory glance at a Bible atlas will show this to be a huge area (in modern terms, taking in Iraq, Jordan, Syria, Lebanon and parts of Turkey). Did Rehum and Shimshai really speak for all these people and all this vast area? It seems highly improbable.

We now get to the letter proper which was copied from the official archives. It is a matchless lesson in toadying to a king. It is worth our while picking out some of the detail, for this will drive the application.

- The letter is enormously pejorative. Jerusalem is called a 'rebellious and wicked city' (v. 12). This slanderous claim is then mixed with facts about the rebuilding work. It is true that the walls are being restored and the foundations repaired. What of it? But, when coupled with the 'rebellious and wicked' assertion, the facts about the building project would become alarming to the king's ear.

- The accusation in the letter also uses spurious arguments – in technical terms, a 'slippery slope argument'. 'If this city is rebuilt and its walls are restored, no more taxes, tribute or duty will be

paid and the royal revenues will suffer' (v. 13).
Now whilst it is true that this *may* be the case, it
is not certainly so – and presenting it as such is
misleading. Moreover, the authors of the letter
use three technical words for tax revenues which
together represent the entirety of the Persian
tax system, a ploy guaranteed to get the king's
attention (which it does, see his replay of the terms
in verse 20). Today, it would be like listing 'income
tax, corporation tax, duty and VAT' – lose all
that and there will no money raised at all! Nor is
this simply a 'slippery slope argument', it contains
exaggeration as well; even if (and it's a big if) taxes
were curtailed, it is surely going too far to say that
'no more' will be paid.

- Verse 14 is somewhat ambiguous. Are Rehum and
  Shimshai really so interested in the king's honour?
  They may be and the 'obligation' they feel may
  be genuine, but seen in the light of the rest of the
  letter this seems highly unlikely. More obviously,
  they are using the king's honour as a shield for
  their own prejudices and desire to oppose the Jews.

- The authors request that a search be made. Fair
  enough. As careful Bible readers we know the kind
  of things a search would turn up: the service of
  Daniel; the efforts of Mordecai to save the king's
  father's life (Esther 6:2); the Jewish ethnicity of
  Esther, the Queen Mother, and the subsequent
  standing of her people (Esther 10:3). But no, all
  these are absent. Instead, what we get is what
  research scientists call *confirmation bias*: if you

know what you're looking for, you very often find it.[14] The king has many, many documents available to him but tell him what to look for and he won't turn up anything else (which is exactly what happens in v. 19). And true enough, there had been times when the city had been 'rebellious' but those times (in Babylonian and Persian history at least) had been relatively rare and easily dealt with.

- That brings us neatly to the last part of the letter which again uses exaggeration to scare the king into action. For if Jerusalem is rebuilt, so the claim goes, 'you will be left with nothing in Trans-Euphrates.' This, again is an extraordinary claim. Even at the height of David and Solomon's reign their territory did not cover this kind of area. Rehum and Shimshai can only justify their huge claim on the basis that Jerusalem was once ruling over a large empire but here too their words are full of hyperbole.

So what are we to make of the inflammatory request in this letter? It serves to show us the schemes of those opposed to God's plans. These enemies of God will use every wile and trick to pursue their cause. They will exaggerate those they represent, make leaps of logic and carefully choose their battles. They will be selective with history and feel no compulsion about exaggerating for effect. The only question is, how will the king respond? We're not going to be surprised at the answer.

---

14. More correctly, confirmation bias 'is a tendency for people to favour information that confirms their preconceptions or hypotheses regardless of whether the information is true.' Taken from the Princeton wiki.

The king's reply (4:17-22)

How does the strategy work with the King? It's a walk-over. The King is drawn comprehensively into the objection and replies with essentially the same arguments that have been made to him. His search turns up exactly what has been suggested he look for (v. 19). At this point the NIV and ESV diverge. Probably the ESV reading is more likely. In both cases Artaxerxes identifies kings to whom the threefold tax revenue was paid. In the case of the NIV these kings were kings *in* Jerusalem. In the case of the ESV these kings were *over* Jerusalem.[15] It seems improbable that Babylonian/Persian records stretched back as far as the times of David (to whom this must refer, *per* NIV) and it is hard to see why the contemporary technical Persian tax words would be used of such an ancient regime. No, more likely the king has discovered that mighty kings were *over* Jerusalem (as the ESV has it) and Jerusalem paid 'taxes, tribute and duty' to them. Cyrus, Cambyses, Darius and Xerxes all benefitted in this way. They are likely to be the mighty kings of verse 20.

Verse 22 indicates that Artaxerxes also believed the opponents' claim that they are writing because they are concerned for the King's honour (v. 14). Artaxerxes is unlikely to be interested in the well-being of Rehum and Shimshai or any other of his officials however important or geographically widespread they may be. No, the king is only interested in the king and the sycophantic nature of the original letter caught his attention just as it was, no doubt, designed to do.

---

15. The Hebrew conjunction *al* can be translated either way.

Conclusion (4:23-24)

So, work must stop (v. 21). Indeed, work was ordered to stop and Rehum and Shimshai were given the warrant they wanted. Unsurprisingly, this is put into action immediately; we're not surprised that the crafty authors of this letter are quick to turn into aggressive enforcers. Verse 23 concludes this story from Artaxerxes' reign and then the author brings us back to the present day with his words about the halt in temple-building (v. 24). As we have seen, this is not to link this standstill directly with the Artaxerxes' letters so many years later, but rather to make the point that it is precisely this *kind* of opposition that led to the closing down of the temple building site.

From text to message

This is another sobering section. We are meant, I believe, to feel some of the injustice of the arguments put to Artaxerxes. The preacher or teacher, therefore, has to work hard to convey the extraordinary nature of the letter and the way it exaggerates and twists logic to win the argument. In this particular case there is no input from the Israelites at all. Humanly speaking they are powerless to stop this false accusation and its outcome.

Getting the message clear: the theme

God's enemies successfully deceive authorities to further their cause.

Getting the message clear: the aim

Like the previous section this passage encourages us to expect opposition and equips us to spot it. We should be unsurprised by unjust accusations, for we follow in the Master's footsteps. Perhaps a key New Testament control would be the text, 'Do not be surprised at the fiery ordeal that has come on you to test you, as though something strange were happening to you. But rejoice inasmuch as you participate in the sufferings of Christ, so that you may be overjoyed when his glory is revealed' (1 Pet. 4:12-13).

It might be theoretically possible to see how Ezra 4 foreshadows the kinds of threats and accusations that Christ Himself faced at trial. For example, how do you get Pilate's interest? 'We have found this man…He opposes payment of taxes to Caesar and claims to be Messiah, a king' (Luke 23:2). Why not exaggerate the threat? 'He stirs up people all over Judea by his teaching' (Luke 23:5). Whilst it is possible to connect all these accusations in Ezra 4 to Jesus directly, it is better to see in the entirety of the false accusations made against Jerusalem, the entirety of the false accusations made against Christ. 'If the world hates you, keep in mind that it hated me first' (John 15:18).

A way in

The passage essentially contains an exchange of letters with which the Israelites have nothing to do. They are not asked for any input nor are they given a chance to defend themselves. It might be useful, therefore, to use a contemporary illustration to show how common this is.

A different way in would be to take people straight to the trial of Jesus. Feeling the injustice of His trial will help us understand our own calling to follow in His footsteps and to bear up under such opposition and entrust ourselves to Him who judges justly (1 Pet. 2:23). Another idea is to begin the sermon or study by introducing the work of our chief enemy. Satan is powerful and crafty but not particularly innovative and the sovereign Spirit has inspired and preserved an exchange of emails here that help us see right into Satan's book of plans. What Christian wouldn't want to take a peek?

Ideas for application

- Opposition is to be constantly expected. There is no let up from those who oppose the work of God. Christ Himself was opposed and we should consider it a blessing to be treated as He was (Luke 6:22-23).

- The enemies of God will use earthly authorities to pursue their goals. Christians should not be surprised when human rulers and authorities are set against the church. Indeed, we should probably expect this to be the norm. Several centuries of 'Christendom' in the West have given many of us a false impression of what Christians should expect from authorities.

- There will be times when there is nothing, humanly speaking, that believers can do about such persecution. Without giving any chance of redress, our enemies will mischievously solicit authorities to stir up trouble for Christians who seem powerless to defend themselves even when the accusations are patently untrue.

- We should expect – and learn to spot – exaggerated claims, leaps of logic and cleverly targeted arguments, together with a deliberate ignoring of the good Christians have done.

- In all the opposition we face we are being counted as Christ. Our joy comes, not from the circumstances of life, but that we are His and we are to count it a privilege to be treated as He was.

- Even if we don't face this particular kind of persecution *now* there are plenty who do and they should be borne up constantly in prayer.

- We need to keep remembering that the text presents this kind of opposition as working (v. 24). This sobering conclusion needs to set the tenor of the passage. Light will come in the next chapter.

Suggestions for preaching

Sermon 1

One sermon might cover the whole of chapter 4. This would allow the preacher to group all the opposition passages together. This approach may be necessary in a shorter series even though inevitably such a sermon couldn't unpack a lot of the detail of the letters. In a sermon that takes the chapter as a whole, the focus should be on the different paths of attack the enemies of God take:

- Opposition against leaders

- Opposition against the people

- Opposition using authorities

It is important to make sure Christological lines are drawn: in this case, the preacher would need to show that God's Son experienced opposition in precisely these ways and that, as His followers, we should expect similar treatment.

Sermon 2

A sermon covering just the second part of the chapter (Ezra 4:6-24) could pick up on more of the details of the letter to Artaxerxes. A close examination of this letter shows the various methods used by those who oppose God and His people.

The enemies of God pursue their cause by:

- **Exaggerating those they represent.** It seems highly improbable that all those listed in verses 9-10 are really signatories to the letter.

- **Making leaps of logic.** Rebuilding Jerusalem did not have to lead to all the tax revenues from the city drying up.

- **Choosing battles carefully.** Most kings are sensitive about income but this was particularly true of Artaxerxes. The letter lays great stress on the prospect of financial ruin and uses a number of technical tax terms to increases the effect. It targets the king's worst fears.

- **Lying about motives.** It is just about possible that the motives of Rehum and Shimshai were honourable but given the context of the letter this seems highly unlikely.

- **Being selective with the facts.** Although an argument from silence, what the letter omits is very noticeable: the positive records of Daniel, Mordecai and Esther for starters. Jews were clearly not all dangerous rebels out to ruin the kings of Persia.

- **Influencing the outcome.** It is no surprise that the king discovers exactly what he is tasked to find.

Having looked at the enemies' strategy in Ezra 4, the preacher can then draw lines to Christ and to us. The text resonates both with the life of Christ *and* with the kind of opposition we face. However, a six-point sermon which traces each kind of opposition, point by point, to Christ and then to us might well be tiresome and repetitive. A better way would be to make the six points from Ezra's account and then show how the whole picture of the enemy's strategy here is echoed in Christ's experience and in ours.

Once again the conclusion needs to reflect verse 24. This kind of opposition works. Artaxerxes is hooked. This sermon – in Christological terms – ends on Good Friday. Easter Sunday is yet to dawn.

Suggestions for teaching

Questions to help understand the passage

1. What is the purpose of including the two short stories of opposition (v. 6-7)?

2. Whom do Rehum and Shimshai claim to represent? How likely is that, do you think?

3. Read their letter to the king. Note down their arguments. How genuine are they? What flaws can you spot in their logic?

4. This is a very selective view of recent history. Who is missing?

5. How does the king's reply reflect the original letter?

6. What is the outcome?

Questions to help apply the passage

1. How does this opposition echo the opposition that Jesus faced? Think particularly of His trial.

2. What does Jesus Himself say about such opposition? Look up John 15:18.

3. How did Jesus face such trials and how should we? Look up 1 Peter 2:23 and 4:12-13.

4. Do you think this means we are to never defend ourselves? If not, what does it mean in practice?

5. How is this passage a help to us as we face opposition?

6. How does it help us pray for Christians around the world?

7. ...Oh, no it doesn't! (Ezra 5:1-6:12)

Introduction

We now come to one of the longest sections in the book, in the way I have divided it up. It's tempting to break this passage into shorter sections – for example, making a break between the letter sent to King Darius (5:1-17) and his favourable reply (6:1-12). However, doing so would disrupt the flow of the text; both parts of this correspondence are needed for the message of the text to sing out. We need to hear this message clearly, a message which stands in sharp contrast to the one conveyed by the exchange of letters in chapter 4. It might be possible to split off 5:1-2 and deal with this section separately. It would be a relatively short, focused sermon, but would be true to the function of these verses and make a strong point about the ministry of the word. I shall suggest an approach below.

At the end of Chapter 4 the author noted that the work on the temple came to a standstill until the second year of Darius' reign. In chapter 5 we learn how the work restarted at that time. We learnt back in 4:1-5 about the opposition which stopped the rebuilding and chronologically chapter 5 picks up the story from there. You will remember that the rest of chapter 4 gave details of separate times of opposition which took place many years after Ezra's time. There we read of letters being exchanged between officials and King Artaxerxes. Now in chapter 5 we read of another exchange of letters between officials and another king, Darius.

Why has the author decided to give us another exchange of letters – clearly mirroring the rather downbeat story in chapter 4? It is because he wants us to see the contrast. Yes, the message of chapter 4 was bleak and rather discouraging:

opposition works. We were meant to feel the pain and sadness of the way that the Lord's work ground to a halt. But though that was the end of *that* story, it is not the end of *the* story – not the story of the Bible in totality nor even the story of rebuilding in Ezra itself. In other words, we're now reading part two of a two-parter. Like a cliff-hanger in a good TV series, by the end of chapter 4 we feel that – despite a good start – there's little hope for the people of Israel. Now, under the sovereign hand of God, we see that there is. Opposition works... (chapter 4) ...oh, no it doesn't! (chapters 5-6).

Why do we need this contrast? Why is chapter 4 needed at all? Could we not have seen the opposition and its techniques without the rather pessimistic ending to the story of Artaxerxes? Could we not have simply been told that opposition is always overcome in the end? There are at least two good reasons why the text is crafted in this way.

First, though we know theologically that all opposition to God and His people will ultimately be defeated, it does not always feel or seem like that now. Scripture is true to the realities of life serving the Lord. His sovereignty is in no way diminished by the work of a powerful enemy who prowls around. Christians need to feel this tension and be aware of how Satan attacks. They need to know that his strategies can seem effective. A happy ending in chapter 4 would have robbed the story of the sobering impact this truth imparts.

Secondly, bringing together these contrasting stories builds the tension and sharpens the contrast. To put it more bluntly, as we read through the exchange of letters in chapters 5 and 6 we are automatically asking the questions: What is so different this time? Isn't this just going to be a re-run of the exchange in chapter 4? If we did not have chapter 4, we might not ask those questions. We might be more inclined to read the interchanges with Darius in chapters 5 and 6 as just another story where the heroes win. Including the chapter 4 story, where the heroes certainly do not win, makes us ask the right questions of the subsequent narrative.

Listening to the text

Context and structure

We are now into the reign of Darius (522 b.c.–486 b.c.) who succeeded Cambyses as King of Persia. Ezra says nothing about Cambyses but we know from history that he was the son of Cyrus. The text's silence about Cambyses is unsurprising, for he was a less famous figure than Cyrus and as such it would not be particularly unusual for him to be counted together with his more notable father. In the latter years of Cambyses' reign his popularity decreased and he was eventually overthrown. Although the actual events are somewhat confused, it is clear that Darius, a warrior, rose to the top of the pile. Antiquity knows him as Darius the Great, a recognition that he ruled over the Persian Empire at its height. Darius came from a different bloodline from Cyrus and so there was no family reason why Darius should honour his predecessor's command; the kings of Persia did, however, see themselves as a continuous line stretching back even before the rise of the Babylonian empire.[16]

The exchange of letters in chapters 5 and 6 is extremely similar to that recorded in chapter 4. Chapter 5 begins with a positive introduction (vv. 1-2) which counteracts the

---

16. This is almost certainly the reason for calling Cyrus/Darius the 'King of Assyria' in Ezra 6:22.

negative end of chapter 4. There follows a preamble to the letters and then the letters themselves. So the structure is straightforward:

- Introduction (5:1-2)

- Preamble to letter (5:3-5)

- Tattenai's letter to Darius (5:6-17)

- Darius' reply to Tattenai (6:1-12)

Working through the text

Introduction (5:1-2)

These first two verses explain how the negative ending to chapter 4 and, more particularly, how the cessation of work because of opposition (4:5,24), is turned around. As such, it might be possible to join 5:1-2 together with chapter 4 (the chapter divisions are not inspired, of course). However, to do so would be to diminish the negative effect that the author wants to create with the carefully constructed Artaxerxes story in 4:7-23.

The point being made in these two verses is clear enough. Work gets restarted because of the 'preaching' of the two contemporary prophets of the time – Haggai and Zechariah, both identified as such and both of whose prophecies have been preserved in the Scriptures. This short section is full of little reminders about the nature of what is going on: we see to whom they prophesy ('the Jews in Judah and Jerusalem'), we see the nature of their calling ('in the name of the God of Israel') and we see another reminder of His sovereign rule ('who was over them'). This 'them' (v. 1) seems most obviously to be a reference to 'the Jews in Judah and Jerusalem.'

Examining the prophecies themselves in the books of Haggai and Zechariah shows that many were spoken directly to the two leaders mentioned in Ezra 5:2 (for example, Joshua in Zech. 3 and Zerubbabel in Zech. 4). It is no surprise therefore that these two men are identified in the recommencement of building (v. 2). After all, they have been instrumental from the beginning (compare Ezra 3).

Two questions arise naturally in our minds from a reading of this passage. First, what is the precise nature of the prophets' ministry? The NIV translates the term used in verse 1 as 'prophesied', but translates the same term in 6:14 as 'preaching' (the ESV translates both as 'prophesied/ prophesying'). The text here is still Aramaic so these words are not common in the Old Testament, given that so little of it is written in Aramaic. We don't therefore have the usual scope for seeking for a clear meaning by looking elsewhere in the Scriptures. The word literally means 'to act the prophet', a noun which itself occurs earlier on in 5:1. In Aramaic the prophet word group means 'one who has the role of speaking for God in revelation or preaching inspired application.'[17] 'Preaching' is therefore an acceptable translation. Haggai and Zechariah have the responsibility of bringing the word of God to the people of God and applying it to their circumstances.

The second question is the precise nature of the help these prophets gave (v. 2). It was clearly related to them being 'on the spot' as we are told that the prophets were 'with them' (Zerubbabel and Jeshua). Some want to make this a picture of the men of God rolling up their

---

17. Swanson, J., *A Dictionary of Biblical Languages: Aramaic* (Bellingham, USA: Logos Research Systems, 1997), entry 10455.

sleeves and getting stuck in physically: perhaps Haggai was handy with the cement mixer? Some rather spurious applications follow! Whilst not wanting to rule out this possibility (or these applications!) the context of the text would seem to suggest that the help the prophets gave here was a continuation of the help they give from the start, that is, bringing God's word. That is confirmed by the prophecies themselves. These prophesies contain careful dating (consistent with other Bible books of this era, not least Ezra itself). The dates reveal that the ministries of Haggai and Zechariah continue over many months: Haggai in a more concentrated period (August–December 520 B.C.) and Zechariah over a longer time (picking up where Haggai left off in 520 B.C. and continuing through to December 518 B.C.). The overall point is well made: the work restarts after the fallow period and it's all down to the ministry of God's word amongst His people.

Preamble to letters (5:3-5)

Before we get to the letters proper we are introduced to the correspondents. Like last time around there are again two officials who initiate events and take the lead, their names are Tattenai and Shethar-Bozenai. Unlike Rehum and Shimshai (4:8), the role of Tattenai at least is much clearer. He was governor of Trans-Euphrates and Shethar-Bozenai was his official (5:6). Rather ironically this pair would have had a greater claim on the wide group that are rather optimistically identified in chapter 4. However, even at this stage we get a clear sense that this present enquiry is going to be different from the previous one: there are no outlandish claims in the preamble nor is there any indication that their questions are anything other than genuine enquiries.

We need to remember that Darius would have been a relatively new king (from the dates of Haggai's and Zechariah's prophecies) and that building work had only just restarted (vv. 1-2). With a new regime in place, Tattenai would have been understandably wary of temple rebuilding happening in places like Jerusalem.

These officials ask two questions of the Jews: first, who authorised the rebuilding? and second, what are the names of those rebuilding? It would be easy for us, especially in the light of chapter 4, to read too much aggression or opposition into these enquiries. But it is clear from the letter that follows that the questions are genuine ones and the response the Jews gave is faithfully recorded and passed on. Contrast this with the previous letter that gave the people of God no opportunity to answer for their actions or defend themselves.

Above all, the insertion of the narrative comment in verse 5 makes it quite clear that we are meant to see this different pattern emerging. Just as the Lord had moved the hearts of the Israelites to start building and sent His prophets to get the work restarted, so now His 'eye' is watching over the elders of the Jews (a more generic term for the leadership, probably similar to 'the heads of the families', see 1:5, 4:2).

Tattenai's letter to Darius (5:6-17)

The narrator tells us that he is about to record a 'copy' of the letter that was sent to the king. No doubt this means he is giving us an official copy from the royal records (confirmed by the continuation of Aramaic in what follows). This is an important detail: it tells us that what we have here is first-hand material. Whilst a Jewish historian is unlikely to fabricate the depressing chapter 4 story, the outcome here is *so* different that there is a real possibility of an accusation of embellishment. The accusation is silenced by providing the royal Xerox.

The letter itself has an entirely different tone to the one we became familiar with last time around. It begins with a factual account of what is going on – building methods and motives. The reference to large stones is thought by some to be an indication of nervousness on the part of Tattenai and Shethar-Bozenai; however, this language is just following the original temple building plan (see 1 Kings 6:36) and so is almost certainly simply descriptive. Verse 9 then accurately records the two questions posed to the Jews in verses 3-4. There is no embellishment or – as we saw last time – loaded comments designed to extract a certain reply from Darius. Rather, there is a letter within a letter as these officials include a detailed reply from the elders of Israel to their two initial enquiries.

In the Jewish reply, the two key questions are answered. However, the Jews answer in a rather roundabout flowery way rather than providing a list of concise bullet points. Why so? In essence, the reply Zerubbabel and Joshua give is a retelling of the Israelites' story. It is important for them to do this because answering the two questions in a straightforward manner might not have been enough to secure the rebuilding work. For example, it would not explain the presence of the many treasures (1:7-11), ready to be placed in a completed temple. Telling the story therefore allows the Jewish leaders to give some background to their situation rather than just giving bald answers: they are showing their workings.

It is reading too much into the text to say that the record of these letters deliberately cuts off some of the accusations made in chapter 4 against the people of God. The letters to Artaxerxes are much later. Nevertheless, we saw in chapter 4 that the later letters are presented as a kind of template of the way opposition works in every age: it should be no surprise therefore if we find that the Jewish leaders' reply includes answers to the types of accusations commonly made against God's people.

The Jews' letter is theological throughout. It begins with a statement of identity that is related to the worship of God.[18] This is more than a simple matter of religious grouping: their relation to the 'God of heaven and earth' (a title used only here in Ezra, although an abbreviated form appears in 6:10) will be essential for explaining the next part of their story, namely how they got to be in Babylon in the first place. Before they address this, though, there is an important point to be made: this temple is not the first to be built. In other words, this is not a temple building programme; it is a temple *rebuilding* programme. The difference is more than semantic as the original edict of Cyrus required the temple to be rebuilt on previous lines (see 6:3). Next we hear an honest assessment of why the Exile took place. This is – at first glance – an unusual matter to include. It does, however, explain why the first temple was destroyed and portrays the returning Exiles as a humbled nation who might be willing – perhaps – to accept the authorities who are now over them. Verses 13-15 then get

---

18. We should not read anything into the absence of the divine name LORD in this letter. The tetragammon does not appear in any of the Aramaic sections of the Old Testament, neither here, nor in Ezra 7:12-26, nor Daniel 2:4–7:28.

to the crux of the matter, essentially summarising chapter 1. The detail in verse 14, 'he *even* removed…' (italics added) is an indication that our approach in chapter 1, where we felt the extraordinary generosity of Cyrus, was the right one.

We might ask whether there is really so much difference between this letter and the one in chapter 4 that was loaded with confirmation bias. Isn't this another example of an attempt to influence the outcome of the search of the royal archives? How is the Jews' letter any more noble than that of their enemies, Rehum and Shimshai? There is a world of difference. Primarily, the Jewish letter does not seek or demand a search for a particular document: it is Tattenai and Shethar-Bozenai who do this (v. 17). Moreover, even if we might see an implication in the Jews' reply that a search should be made, the plea from the Jews is quite different, coming as it does in a letter that honestly establishes the nation as rebels being justly punished.[19]

Having said all this, we have to admit that the last statement of the Jews is stretching the truth a little! 'From that day to the present it has been under construction, but is not yet finished.' This statement could certainly be seen as true on one level but it ignores the fact that the building work has been largely fallow for a decade or more. Since the point of the letter is to establish a continuity with the work begun in the reign of Cyrus we should not overstate this slight embellishment, if indeed that is the way we should see it.

The letter closes with a straightforward plea from the officials asking the king to see if such an edict really does

---

19. For notes on Sheshbazzar as governor and layer of the foundation, see p. 90.

exist. One small detail is worth picking out. Tattenai and his associates ask for a search to be made in Babylon, the empire's capital. We will soon discover that the edict is discovered in an entirely different location. Once again, the Lord's sovereignty will work things out in remarkable ways.

Darius' reply to Tattenai (6:1-12)

Even though the search was in the treasury at Babylon we learn that the relevant scroll was found in the citadel of Ecbatana, a fact that the author is at pains to point out. Surely the 'eye of their God' is indeed 'watching over' the Jews (5:5). Ecbatana was the capital of Media, a significant province incorporated into the Persian Empire before the conquest of Babylon so that it was sometimes called the Empire of the 'Medes and the Persians' (see Dan. 5:28). Ecbatana was one of the known royal residences: 'Cyrus lived in Babylon during the winter, in Susa in the spring, and in Ecbatana in the summer. He resided in Ecbatana the first summer as king of Babylon.'[20] We should not be surprised that royal archives were kept at each location; we should however be surprised that Darius took the trouble to make a more extensive search than that requested. The reply Darius gives includes the content of the document found in the archives and is based upon its evidence.

Our next surprise is in the content of the scroll[21] that was discovered. It begins with a rather modern sounding word, 'memorandum' (ESV, 'a record'). This word however,

---

20. Breneman, M., *Ezra, Nehemiah, Esther* (Nashville, US: Broadman & Holman, 1993), p. 114.

21. Although many documents of the time were recorded in clay, these tend to be the ones that are extant, for obvious reasons. There is plenty of evidence to show that scrolls were also used.

represents the exact nature of what was found – a copy of the edict (which begins in v. 3b), prefaced by a preamble (that was written at the same time as the edict) giving details for the court records. This preamble confirms the dating we saw in 1:1, the 'first year of King Cyrus.'

The edict itself is similar but not identical to the one in chapter 1. Indeed, it adds new details. Before we get to the details themselves we must ask whether these two accounts can or should be harmonised. First, we need to say that the two edicts appear to have different foci: the chapter 1 command includes reference to the return of the Jews themselves as well as to the rebuilding of the temple. This second edict makes no mention of the people and it includes more detail about how the rebuilding of the temple is to be financed and also about the temple's dimensions.

Such differences should not surprise us. The return of exiled people was a matter of great significance for a conquering empire and could not be achieved by a few lines on a single clay tablet. There would have been all kinds of issues to resolve that would require different officials and ministries. In short, what we appear to have discovered in chapter 6 is the Treasury version of the edict, a document which answered the key question: how is this rebuilding going to be paid for? The two edicts are complementary therefore rather than contradictory.

And we should thank God that both edicts are included in Ezra, for the first confirms to us that the Lord's hand is upon the temple rebuilding and the second amplifies the extraordinary nature of God's condescension. For here in this Persian Treasury memo we discover that the royal coffers will pay for the rebuilding of the temple (v. 4).[22] Moreover, we gain more information about Cyrus' actions in 1:7-11 where he returns the temple treasures to the returning Jews. Back in chapter 1 Cyrus seemed to be a generous benefactor – now we discover a little more. He rules that the temple articles must be returned 'to their places' (a phrase that in essence occurs in the text of the Cyrus Cylinder). Cyrus is a religious pluralist and his ruling here reflects religious thought of the time: for worship to be in any way acceptable to a god or gods it had to be conducted exactly in the manner prescribed by that particular religion.

Verse 5 marks the end of the memorandum though the NIV text does not make this clear. From verse 6 onwards the voice speaking is that of the current king, Darius, who takes and amplifies the already-generous edict of his predecessor. We might have thought that the Jews could never find a better benefactor than Cyrus, but as we read on we find that Darius not only confirms Cyrus' generosity but also actually extends it.

First, Darius orders Tattenai and his associates to keep away from the building site, they are not to 'interfere'. This is no more than an application of the Cyrus edict. However, Darius then issues an additional instruction: these officials are to help out, thus reversing the natural role of Tattenai as governor over the Israelites. Darius is very explicit in terms of the help that is to be given: it is not direct building help (of the kind that Zerubbabel has rejected in 4:1-3). Rather:

---

22. A detail which derails the argument that the reduced glory of the second temple was because the Jews could not afford to build it as before, a view which is sometimes expressed to explain the tears in 3:12-13. For comments on dimensions, see comments on 3:7-13.

- All expenses are to be paid out of the local budget (v. 8b). Although it might be argued that this is no more than Cyrus ordered (v. 4b), the language is more explicit both in terms of the amount ('fully paid' against 'paid') and its source ('from the revenues of Trans-Euphrates').

- In verse 9 we learn that animals and produce are to be provided so that offerings may be given at the temple. We are not to read too much into this: it says nothing about the religious convictions of Darius other than – like other kings of the time – he was a confirmed pluralist. Nor are Darius' motives anything other than self-centred. These offerings are to be given for the health and wealth of the royal family (v. 10). Some commentators wonder whether there may have been some Jewish input into the content and wording of this decree; the precise language of sacrifice might suggest so. This would be quite possible as we know that not all Jews had left Babylon (cf. Esther) and some could have been in royal service.

- Darius is so keen for the work to be completed that he will commit not only financial resources but protection as well. Verses 11-12 are rather gruesome but portray a kind of 'eye for eye' retributive punishment which was typical of the day. If anyone tries to undo the work of the building of God's house, they themselves will be

undone by their own house.[23] It is important to
note that this edict only related to temple building
and so could not be called upon during the
Artaxerxes crisis (4:8-23).

So ends a quite different exchange of letters. Tattenai and
Shethar-Bozenai have acted honourably and there is no
reason to suppose that they will do anything other than
implement Darius' decree diligently, just as he asks (v. 12b).

From text to message

Getting the message clear: the theme
God sovereignly uses His word to restart the building work
and uses His power abundantly to provide for His work.

Getting the message clear: the aim
The passage encourages us with two key messages, both
about the sovereign hand of God. On the one hand
there is the work of the word of God which gets the
building restarted and in which God's people need to
have confidence. On the other is the providential hand of
God behind the scenes ensuring that even pagan kings are
abundantly disposed towards God's people.

We need to be careful not to make this latter point
into an inviolable rule. After all, this chapter comes hot
on the heels of chapter 4. Rather, the application is in the
contrast with that depressing chapter. Opposition may
seem to work but in the end God's abundant sovereignty
overcomes every enemy, providing all that is needed for
His work to be completed. Preachers and teachers need

23. Derek Kidner points out that this punishment is not unique to the
Bible. Kidner, D., *Ezra and Nehemiah: an introduction and commentary*
(Nottingham, UK: Inter-Varsity Press, 1979), p. 64.

to be cautious about promising to people *now* what God does not promise *until the end*. Nevertheless, it often turns out that the very things that we think may work against us turn out to be for our good and our blessing (Rom. 8:28).

Thinking Christologically, it seems most sensible to see the difference the word makes in terms of the incarnate Word, Jesus Christ. The word (small 'w') of God is still effective today because of the person of whom it speaks, the Word (capital 'W'). Although at first it might seem more difficult to trace the second application to Christ, it too is a natural fit. For the days of mourning that were brought about by the cross turned out to be for our abundant good as Christ was raised and vindicated.

A way in

Having just read the previous exchange of letters (chapter 4) readers should experience at first a certain sense of déjà vu – a sort of 'here we go again'. Surely this is just more of the same? One way in would be to play on this narrative technique of putting apparently similar events next to each other to highlight where they actually differ; the contrast makes the point. So even before the Bible reading you could ask, 'Have you ever begun to read a story where you think you already know the ending? Listen to this story and see, based on last time, how you think it is going to end?' Such questions would build some suspense, a suspense that is there in the text. Of course this story ends quite differently and *abundantly* differently.

As I read all through Ezra I can't help but think of William Cowper's superb hymn on God's providence: 'God moves in a mysterious way.' Perhaps verse 3 is the most pertinent section:

> You fearful saints, fresh courage take;
> the clouds you so much dread
> are big with mercy, and shall break
> in blessings on your head.[24]

This verse captures the encouragement we can take from the surprise twist in our passage; that whilst events may appear to just be more of the same, under God nothing may be further from the truth.

Ideas for application

- It is the word of God proclaimed which gets the building work restarted and also sustains it. We need to keep reminding ourselves of the centrality of the ministry of the word in kingdom life alongside the importance of raising up and supporting gospel workers who bring the word to us.

- The prophecies of Haggai and Zechariah (the latter in particular) are Christological. The preached word must bring us to Christ – He is our great motivation in the building work, for He is the Chief Cornerstone.

- We see again the abundant generosity of God in providing for His people all that they need, sometimes from some very surprising places. This is the doctrine of providence in action. We should rejoice that God is working His purposes out even though this is not always visible to us.

---

24. *God moves in a mysterious way* by William Cowper (1731-1800).

- Chapter 4 showed us that we must expect opposition and cannot presume on support from those who don't know God; nevertheless, in God's sovereign goodness neither should we be surprised when He uses remarkable means to support His work of kingdom building.

Suggestions for preaching

Sermon 1

A brief sermon might pick up on the first two verses. It would be narrowly focused but could connect well with the previous section which ended with apparent defeat.

- **The ministry of the word is key to rebuilding.** This point is about the content of what was said and its authorisation ('in the name of the God of Israel who was over them').

- **The ministers of the word are key to rebuilding.** This is a slightly different point about those the ascended Christ Jesus gives to His church to serve those who are called to build.

Sermon 2

A better sermon would keep all the material of this section together, given that the author's main point here is to show how the temple building came to be completed. Of the two points that I list below the second is given much more time in the text and the preacher would need to reflect this in his content and approach.

- **God's kingdom is built through the ministry of the word** (5:1-2). This point would combine the issues outlined above in *Sermon 1.*

- **God's kingdom is built through His providential rule of all things** (5:3-6:12). This point could be broken down into two and a separate heading given to 5:11-17 which reflects that '**God's kingdom is built through faithful and honest servants.**'

These headings are applicatory, that is, they contain the application lessons of the sermon. Choosing headings that retell the passage would almost certainly be unnecessary as the story is self-explanatory. Preachers need, however, to be careful they retain the colour and surprise of the passage when they are explaining and applying.

It would also be possible to include 6:13-15 (which completes the story of the rebuilding) in this section as it provides a useful summary of the points outlined above.

Suggestions for teaching
Questions to help understand the passage

1. What happened to the building project at the end of chapter 4?

2. Which two characters get the work restarted? Who are they and what do they do?

3. Tattenai begins by asking the elders of the Jews what they are doing. Read their response (5:11-17). What do you notice about it?

4. How is Tattenai's letter to King Darius different from the letter that we read in chapter 4?

5. How does Darius respond?

6. What are the similarities between this decree (6:3-5) and the one in chapter 1? What are the differences?

Questions to help apply the passage

1. What place does the ministry of the word have in kingdom building today? How can we ensure that this is not lost?

2. What place do ministers of the word have in kingdom building today? What can we do to encourage this ministry?

3. What does the elders' response teach us about honest self-evaluation? How can we apply this to life in the church?

4. How does the exchange of letters between Tattenai and Darius encourage us? Can we always assume God will act this way? How do we know? (Think back to chapter 4.)

5. What do the surprises of the chapter teach us about the way God works in the world and in His kingdom?

6. Go back to 4:24. We left that chapter negatively. How do these following chapters help correct that view?

8. Finishing with a feast (Ezra 6:13-22)

Introduction

The first half of the book now closes with two appropriate summaries. The first (in vv. 13-18) describes the completion of the temple and its dedication. The second (in vv. 19-22) narrates the first Passover to be celebrated in the Second Temple era. Both these summaries have a strong focus on the means by which these events came about: in the first the emphasis is on the combination of God's sovereignty and earthly decree; in the second section the text emphasises that the joy the Israelites felt came from God Himself.

Listening to the text

Context and structure

Both these closing stories have close links with what has gone before. In particular, the language of verses 13-14 reinforces the lessons that have been made in the previous section (in fact they almost act as a control for rightly understanding that story). It is the preaching of the word of God by the two prophets, combined with the decrees of the kings (themselves under God's sovereignty) which has led to the temple's completion. The exact date stamp (we would translate it as 12 March 515 B.C.) marks the significance of the moment.

The festival celebrated at the start of the building project was the Feast of Tabernacles (3:4), a festival that commemorated wandering in the wilderness. The Passover (6:19) helped the Israelites remember their salvation from slavery in a faraway country and so as with the Feast of

Tabernacles in chapter 3 it is entirely appropriate that the author highlights the Passover to close this section.

The passage splits obviously into two:

- Finishing the Temple (6:13-18)
- Celebrating the Passover (6:19-22)

Working through the text

Finishing the Temple (6:13-18)

This first section provides a link to the previous story of Darius' edict and concludes the temple building narrative with a record of its dedication. The construction project will now disappear from the story. In one short paragraph we are reminded of all the factors which contributed to getting the temple finished.

First, we learn that the officials who wrote the chapter 5 letter, Tattenai and Shethar-Bozenai, carry out the king's decree 'with diligence.' This is an extraordinary turnaround from the situation outlined in chapter 4 where opponents of the nation used their leverage with the king to try to halt the work. Now, as we have already seen, the king orders that the Governor actually assist the work and this to his credit is exactly what he does.

Many commentators rightly see in this a further example of the doctrine of providence. It would have been quite possible, given the distance between Jerusalem and Babylon, for Tattenai to find other ways to frustrate the work. Yet in God's sovereignty he dutifully does what has been asked of him by the king.

We are then reminded that the 'elders of the Jews' (representing the nation) 'continued to build and prosper under the preaching of Haggai the prophet and Zechariah, a descendant of Iddo.' The further reference to the two prophets bookends the story recorded in chapters 5 and 6 and ensures we do not lose sight of what is going on. Lest we think that the rebuilding is all down to Tattenai's intervention, this little clause puts us right. It is the preaching of Haggai and Zechariah that not only has got the work restarted (5:1-2) but has also ensured that it is completed.

The summary sentence that follows brings together God's work and the kings' actions: 'They finished building the temple according to the command of the God of Israel and the decrees of Cyrus, Darius and Artaxerxes, kings of Persia.' A careful reader might wonder why Artaxerxes gets a mention here. After all, the temple was completed long before he came to reign and it was only the decrees of Cyrus and Darius that made a positive difference. However, the author is almost certainly tying up all the loose ends from this first section, and seeing as he has introduced a long opposition section from the reign of Artaxerxes in chapter 4, it seems appropriate to include him in the list. We need to know that even when things are not going to plan the sovereign God is still working His purposes out.

As a result of all this it is hardly surprising that the entire nation celebrates the temple's dedication – this last word is *annuka* in Aramaic, later to become a Jewish festival (Hanukah) to mark the temple's rededication in later history (165 B.C.). The offerings are costly and significant but nothing like those of Solomon's day (compare v. 17 with 1 Kings 8:63), a further reminder that though this temple project has been a remarkable one it is not a restoration of the David-Solomon glory days.

The date of reconstruction marks almost seventy years since the destruction of the temple in 586 B.C. although the text makes nothing of this gap (see notes on 1:1). Solomon's temple lasted just under four centuries; this second temple will last until it is destroyed by the Romans in A.D. 70 (though it was renovated by Herod before the birth of Jesus).

One detail warrants further explanation. The dedication includes a 'sin offering for all Israel' (v. 17). It must be remembered that the returning exiles represent just the two southernmost tribes, Judah and Benjamin (see introductory notes). Why then is this offering made for all Israel, an offering that was made up of 'twelve male goats, one for each of the tribes of Israel'?

Surely it is because those who were there that day are now all that's left of Israel; this righteous remnant now represents the continuation of God's promises to His people, promises that will be ultimately fulfilled in Jesus Christ, great David's greater son. In other words, this conclusion to part one of the Ezra story not only looks back but also looks forward in anticipation to what is still to come.

We might wonder why this section is worth considering in isolation from the section immediately before it (chapter 5 and the earlier part of chapter 6). After all, it seems to be dealing with similar material. But there is a subtle change of focus here. In the earlier account, the impact of the preaching of the word of God and the decree of the king was focused entirely on the building project (e.g. the effect of the prophets' preaching in 5:2 and Darius' words in 6:7).

Now the same providential hand sees the temple complete *so that worship can be offered there*. We learn that the climax of the story is not actually the temple itself but the purpose for which it was built. The conclusion in verse 18 is therefore entirely appropriate and significantly does not mention the temple at all.

Celebrating the Passover (6:19-22)

The text now reverts to Hebrew – an appropriate switch of languages, given that this is a description of the Passover celebrations and Persian King Darius has nothing at all to do with this. In Israel's story Passover celebrations often identified key moments in salvation history. The first Passover enabled the Israelites to escape Egypt. The second marked their leaving of Sinai (Num. 9).[25] As we have already seen, the return of the exiles had obvious echoes of the first Exodus so it is highly appropriate to conclude this part of the Ezra story with a celebration of the Passover.

In fact verse 21 hints that more joined in the party than just those who had originally returned and been listed in chapter 2. We should not forget that some twenty-three years have passed since that list was compiled and so it is not surprising that the company of faithful believers has swelled. Although there will be a later group of exiles who return (see chapter 8), some Jews might well have lived within reach of Jerusalem and made their way back independently. Perhaps most significantly this might have included some who had been re-settled in the northern kingdom and had become disillusioned with the mixed up religion they experienced there (see notes on 4:1). If so this would explain the author's inclusion of the description

---

25. Also the defeat of Jericho (Josh. 5) and the renewal of the covenant under King Josiah (2 Kings 23).

'together with all who had separated themselves from the unclean practices of their Gentile neighbours in order to seek the Lord, the God of Israel' (v. 21).

This newly enlarged – though still small – nation comes together and celebrates the Feast of Unleavened Bread (a seven-day period which incorporated the Passover, see Deut. 16:1-8). However, the editorial comment in verse 22 draws our attention to the precise nature of what is happening. Unsurprisingly perhaps, the people are filled with joy. Why wouldn't they be! They are back home after a long exile. The temple is rebuilt. Things are looking up. Yet even now the author is at pains to point out the source of this joy. The people celebrate with joy (see also verse 16) because 'the Lord had filled them with joy by changing the attitude of the king of Assyria,[26] so that he assisted them in the work on the house of God, the God of Israel.'

From text to message
Despite the close connection with the previous passage these two sections are best taken separately as representing the conclusion of Part One of Ezra. In particular, they drive us to see clearly the purpose of the providence of God: God's purpose is to make it possible for His people to worship Him and to fill them with joy in that worship.

---

26. This is a strange title for Cyrus or Darius. The Assyrian empire is long gone and their time is the time of the Babylonians (originally) or the Medes and Persians (see description in 6:14). Why introduce the Assyrian empire here? We cannot be sure, but perhaps it is because it was the Assyrians with whom all the trouble began – whether it is the scattering of the northern kingdom or the vicious attacks by Sennecharib against the southern kingdom which then precipitated all the trouble with Babylon. Perhaps this is the author's way of saying 'That's all behind us now'?

Getting the message clear: the theme
God's sovereign hand enables His people to worship Him with joy.

Getting the message clear: the aim
God's sovereign rule is not aimless, He works in the world to bring about His purposes which are always for our good. More exactly, He enables His people to come to Him. In Old Testament times, this was impossible without the temple in place so that sacrifices could be made. The focus on temple rebuilding turns out to be a staging post on the way to the goal of acceptable worship being offered to God in accordance with the Law of Moses. This is God's doing and He brings joy to His people by making it happen.

There is a clear Christological line here, for in the death and resurrection of Christ God enables us to come to Him. He ordered even the crucifixion of His own Son and continues to order events today to this end. Our salvation is dependent upon His providential hand, both in the events of Calvary and also in the circumstances of our own lives. Such a providential working should fill us with joy.

A way in
The passage is answering the fundamental question, 'What was behind it all?' A good opening would engage the hearer with questions which raise this issue. However, perhaps an even stronger way to begin a sermon on this passage would be to paint a picture of just how far the Israelites had come in twenty-three years. They start the book of Ezra a broken, incarcerated people far from home. Their temple system (on which the Law of Moses depended) looked dead and buried. And yet here just a few years later

they are celebrating the Passover after dedicating the new temple. How did it happen?

Ideas for application

- God's sovereign rule is not an abstract power or force. It is focused on His people (see also Eph. 1:22-23 and Eph. 3:20-21). Moreover, even this focus has a key purpose behind it: the Lord longs that His people might come to Him to worship Him and He enables this to happen.

- The same twin foci of the last section are in view again here. It is the ministry of the word and God's 'behind the scenes' overruling that enables this worship to happen.

- The details of this temple dedication and the temple's need for sacrifices remind us that though this is a glorious moment, these are not yet the glory days of the past nor those promised by Ezekiel in his latter chapters. For example, there is no descent of the glory of God on to the temple and the sacrifices offered pale into insignificance when compared with Solomon's dedication in 1 Kings 8:63.

- The temple dedication represents a return (for the moment) to the operation of the Mosaic Covenant (v. 18) which Jeremiah – writing in exile – has already declared obsolete (see, for example, Jer. 31:31ff.).

- The Passover is an appropriate way to end this section, representing as it does God's rescue of His people from slavery. This festival looks forward too especially in its need to be repeated regularly alongside the daily and special sacrifices.

- The work of God amongst His people draws others in. God's work to bring His people to worship Him has a magnetic effect on those who surround them.

- In this rescue and God's work in it there is a foreshadowing of the rescue we enjoy in Christ Jesus.

- When we understand what God is doing in the world and has done for us in Christ, our hearts should be filled with joy that God should look upon us so favourably.

Suggestions for preaching

Sermon 1

The preacher has a number of options here. First, he could group 6:13-18 together with the previous section in which case the twin foci of the **preaching of the word of God** and the **providential hand of God** (both in verse 14) would no doubt be the two main headings. However, whilst being a natural fit, these concluding verses do seem to have a different thrust when included with verses 16-18.

Sermons 2 & 3

A second and third sermon might deal with these two sections as a separate unit. A slower series on Ezra might be able to accommodate such a pace. The first sermon would reinforce the points made previously and draw the listeners' attention to the purpose of rebuilding the temple.

The second sermon would pick up on the Passover celebration and show again how God's rescue had been affected, anticipating a greater rescue in Christ.

However, there is possibly not quite enough material to sustain two separate sermons: the first would repeat a lot of what was said in the previous section and the second would have to digress into the history and significance of the Passover. This may be no bad thing with a congregation who are largely ignorant of the facts.

In my view a better way forward would be to incorporate both sections together thus:

Sermon 4
This sermon brings the first part of Ezra to a close.

- **The purpose of God: to enable us to worship Him** (6:13-18). This point picks up on the narrow focus of God's sovereign working in the world which is to enable people to worship Him – here under the operation of the Old Covenant. The fact that no glory descends is a reminder that this description is still looking forward to a better day.

- **The response to God: overflowing joy at our rescue** (6:19-22). Once we know that God has enabled us to come to Him, our response should be to celebrate with joy. With godly hindsight we can see how He does indeed work all things for our good (Rom. 8:28) and He fills us with joy as we grasp this truth.

Suggestions for teaching
Questions to help understand the passage

1. The passage reiterates the two factors that have enabled the temple to be rebuilt. What are they?

2. What is odd about the inclusion of Artaxerxes (in verse 14)? Why might his name have been added?

3. Look up the first dedication of the temple (1 Kings 8:1-11, 62-66). What is different this time around and what does that teach us about what is happening?

4. Which covenant is in operation (see verse 18)? Why does this matter?

5. What events in Israel's history does the Passover remind us of and why is this an appropriate ending to the first part of Ezra?

6. Who has joined the returning exiles?

7. Why are the people joyful?

Questions to help apply the passage

1. The temple serves a greater purpose. It was not just a building. What was this purpose and why does this focus help us today when it comes to understanding God's sovereignty?

2. How does this first part of Ezra, concluding it the way it does, help us think about times when things appear not to go our way?

3. Why is there a focus on the sin offering and what does this make us think of today?

4. How should we understand the Passover in the sweep of the whole Bible?

5. Why do you suppose more people had joined the exiles? What does this teach us?

6. Where does the people's joy come from? What then should we do if don't feel very joyful as believers?

THE SECOND RETURN (EZRA 7–10) (458 B.C.–457 B.C.)

1. Introducing Ezra (Ezra 7:1-10)

Breaking the story

We now come to the second part of the story. This is where Ezra himself comes on the scene and this first section introduces him. The original readers/hearers would have been well aware that this chapter jumps forward in time from the end of chapter 6 as this is clearly heralded in verse 1 with the words 'during the reign of Artaxerxes.' In fact, the precise date markers in verse 8 (see below) indicate a gap between 6:22 and 7:1 of just under sixty years.

It is good for the preacher to give hearers some idea of this time gap. Much has clearly taken place during these intervening years. Perhaps most significant in terms of the people of God is the story of Esther who was married to Xerxes, Artaxerxes' predecessor. It is also helpful to make clear that this second part of Ezra is closely associated with the events of the book of Nehemiah. Nehemiah, Artaxerxes' cupbearer, returned to Jerusalem to rebuild its walls just over a decade after Ezra arrived. There are a number of similarities between these two men: both had close relationships with the king and both are said to have had God's hand on them (Ezra 7:6, Neh. 2:8b).

The break in time between the two parts of Ezra is mirrored by a shift in the book's focus of concern – a shift away from the worship that will be offered at the rebuilt temple and towards the holy lives to which God's people are called. Indeed, this will be the presenting issue in the second half of the book, a fact that is heralded by the king's decree (see next section) that Ezra is to ensure that the whole Law is kept. No doubt this is also the reason why Ezra's commitment to the Law is made so explicit in verse 10.

Nevertheless, it is also possible for the preacher to go overboard in seeking to help his hearers appreciate the gap in time. It would be a mistake in my view to break a series on Ezra at the end of chapter 6 and insert a short series on Esther before continuing with Ezra 7 even though this would be chronologically accurate. The Holy Spirit has inspired the assembly of the text as well as its context and he has given us Ezra as one complete book even though it contains this significant break.

Introduction
Chapter 7:1-10 introduces the key figure of Ezra after whom the book is named. He is a priest-teacher and as such he is well suited to the task he will be given of reforming the Law-keeping of the returned exiles.

Listening to the text
Context and structure
This short section is worth taking on its own as it is focused on introducing our main character. Even though the book

is named after him, it is quite probable that Ezra was not even born when the events of chapter 1 took place around eighty years before. It is important, however, to see that the two halves of the story belong together, for the worship of God (through the rebuilt temple) must be accompanied by godly living in accordance with His Law. The phrase 'the Law' or 'the Law of Moses' appears nine times in this second section, eight of them in chapter 7 alone.

The section can be split into:

- Introducing Ezra (vv. 1-6)

- Introducing Ezra's companions (v. 7)

- Introducing Ezra's motivation (vv. 8-10)

In the introduction to this second return (which runs up to the end of the book), there are clear echoes of the first:

- The sovereign hand of God behind the scenes (v. 6 and v. 9, also 7:28, compare 1:1,5)

- A decree from the king, including financial provision (7:13-26, compare 1:2-4)

- A list of those returning to Jerusalem from Babylon (8:1-14, compare 2:1-67)

- Problems with those returning (9:15 – lack of Levites, compare 2:61-63)

Working through the text

Introducing Ezra (vv. 1-6)

'After these things' sounds a rather casual way to mark a long period of time. We should not read too much into the phrase though, because it is accompanied by the time marker 'during the reign of Artaxerxes, king of Persia.'

Artaxerxes reigned from 465 B.C. to 424 B.C. after his father Xerxes (who was married to Queen Esther). There is no indication however that Artaxerxes was one of Esther's children.

The text then introduces Ezra by detailing his lineage. This was relatively unusual for a priest, though key to ascertaining Ezra's credibility, especially in the light of the issues that arose over this matter with the first group who returned. Some of them could not prove their lineage (see 2:61-63) and so were prevented from serving. If Ezra is going to ensure that the people are living according to the Law then his lineage must not be in question.

The lineage recorded here is hugely impressive. The priest of the first section, Joshua, son of Jozadak (2:2), does not receive such attention even though he is the High Priest (see Zech. 3:1). Nowhere is Ezra identified with this title though he is descended from a long line of those who are: Zadok (v. 2) was the High Priest during the high point of Israel's nationhood (when David and Solomon were king); Phinehas and Eleazar feature significantly in the book of Numbers (e.g. Num. 25:6-13); the line we read of here traces all the way back to Aaron himself.[1] It is 'this Ezra' the text is presenting (as opposed to any other that may spring to mind!).

However, despite this lineage of High Priests, the author is more concerned to show us that Ezra is a *teacher* rather than an *intermediary*.[2] The NIV 'teacher' (ESV 'scribe') captures the essence of what his role entailed

---

1. 'Son of' is better translated 'descendent' as there are clearly missing generations. The author has identified key names for us to make a point about Ezra himself.

2. Both are part of a priest's role – see Malachi 2:1-9.

(see verse 10). Ezra is 'well versed in the Law of Moses', a short statement that presents two key facts: first, Ezra's knowledge is considerable – he is no novice; second, his special subject is the Law of Moses. This latter emphasis will become key. We might expect the king to send a specialist in the law of the Medes and Persians (Dan. 6:8) but – as the decree will make clear – he also needs local religious specialists and Ezra fits the bill.

This short section ends with a reference to God again being at work, 'The king granted him everything he asked, for the hand of the Lord was upon him.' The second 'him' is almost certainly Ezra (i.e. God's hand was on Ezra rather than on the king) as is reflected in Ezra's personal testimony in 7:28.[3] As readers we are likely to be surprised to learn that Artaxerxes, the king who opposed the rebuilding of Jerusalem in chapter 4, is now helping Ezra. I will address this in a later section.

The statement that the king granted Ezra's requests does however raise a question. What exactly did Ezra ask for? Later we will discover that he actually refuses to ask the king for help though he undoubtedly could have done so (see 7:21). Therefore it seems much more likely that Ezra sought permission for some more Jews to go home and the king's decree in 7:13-26 is written as an endorsement of Ezra's desire. In this sense Ezra is much more like Nehemiah. In other words, the teacher of the Law is not just interested in its theological or historical implications: he wants to see it lived out by God's people – an idea that will be reinforced in verse 10.

---

3. It is simply too much to read into the text that 7:6 refers to the king and 7:9/28 refers to Ezra, reflecting the emphases in 1:1 and 1:5 on the king and the people respectively.

We must not let these details detract from the close
link the author wants us to see between the human success
of the mission and the sovereign hand of God upon His
servant.

Introducing Ezra's companions (v. 7)
We are now briefly introduced to Ezra's travelling companions. They will be described by name in 8:1-14 and
by role in 8:15-36 but for now it is sufficient to see that
Ezra was accompanied by 'priests, Levites, musicians,
gatekeepers and temple servants' – exactly the same roles
that were highlighted in chapter 2.

Some readers of Ezra wonder why these individuals did
not return in the first tranche, assuming that they were
somehow less spiritual or needed others to take the plunge
before they followed on. But such a reading ignores the
time gap we have already identified. Like Ezra it is highly
unlikely that any of these people were actually alive at the
time of the first return.

Introducing Ezra's motivation (vv. 8-10)
The last three verses continue the description but with a
shift back to Ezra himself. It is 'his' journey rather than
the journey of the combined company. The journey itself
is identified by two precise date markers:

- The 'first day of the first month' is, in modern
  terms, 8 April 458 b.c.

- The 'first day of the fifth month' is equivalent to 4
  August 458 b.c.

The actual journey took less time than this but the arrival
was delayed by Ezra hunting around for additional Levites
(see 8:15, 31). In all the journey took three and a half

months to cover a distance of what experts think was about nine hundred miles.[4]

In verse 9 the author repeats the statement about the providential hand of God being on Ezra and then explicitly links this to Ezra's desire to be a man of the Law. The 'for' at the beginning of verse 9 is significant and is reproduced in most English translations.[5]

This devotion is more literally translated 'set his heart on' which picks up on the sentiment of 1:5. This whole-heartedness is expressed in three areas, all linked and significantly ordered:

- First, Ezra is devoted to the 'study' of the Law. The language implies strong enquiry. In other words, he wants to know what 'the Law of the Lord' *says* and – we might imply from Nehemiah 8:8 – what it *means*. This is more then than simply acquiring knowledge.

- Second, he is devoted to its observance or as the ESV puts it more literally 'to do it.' Ezra's first commitment after understanding the Law is to apply it to himself.

- Third, Ezra is devoted to 'teaching its decrees and statutes in Israel.' Knowing and obeying the Law precedes teaching it to others and necessarily leads to it. We should not read too much into the

---

4. Though the distance 'as the crow flies' is considerably shorter (perhaps 500 miles), travel from Babylon to the West had to be undertaken in a large circular path to avoid the inhabitable deserts. See Fensham, p. 100.

5. Though not in the *New Century Version*. The *Christian Standard Bible* translates it as 'now' which is grammatically possible, though seems to miss the significance of the placement of verse 10.

language of 'decrees and statutes': the words are
used as repeating synonyms to make a point (see
Ps. 119:1-8 where this is also done).

This last verse captures the essence of Ezra's mission and
will shape the rest of the book's message.

Christological interpretation

It is perhaps worth pausing here and asking how we apply
such a passage into a New Covenant context today. It is
quite possible to pick out verse 10 and preach it in isolation
to a congregation (and I will suggest a way of doing that
below). Such a sermon however ignores the historical
context that the author gives to Ezra's mission and also the
crucial role of the providential hand of God. Moreover,
drawing a direct line is impossible as no Christian is called
to obey the 'Law of Moses' in quite the way that Ezra was.

Perhaps another way of preaching the passage would be to
try to be more faithful to the context and see in Ezra a model
of the pastor-teacher today. Such a text would be ideal for a
commissioning service for a new minister or – as I have taught
it myself – a commencement address at a training college.

However, even though such an approach seems to be
more faithful to the context of Ezra himself it still leaves
something to be desired. As with the first approach there is
still work to be done to move from Old Testament Law to
New Testament 'word of God' type applications. Moreover,
it is inescapable in the text that Ezra is a priest. The author
is at pains to point this out. And so applications which jump
straight from Ezra to us (even as preachers and teachers)
still do not reflect the entire Bible context.

A better approach in my view is to see in Ezra a foreshadowing of Christ. He is the Great High Priest and

whilst an exposition of this role is limited to the book of Hebrews and focused on His sacrificing Himself, it is that same book which has as a major theme that the Word of God is still speaking today (see Heb. 1:1-2).

In other words, in our whole-Bible theology the priestly roles of intermediary and teacher[6] come together in Christ Jesus. He is the One who perfectly understood the Law (see for example, Luke 2:46-47); who delighted to do His Father's will (e.g. Heb. 10:7) and taught it to others. The Lord's hand was upon Him as a result. It is because Ezra points us towards Christ that we have in Ezra 7 applications for us today – not only for congregations as a whole but also for those who are particularly set aside for Christian ministry.

Such an approach might seem somewhat 'clunky' or forced (and at worst it could be presented in a very artificial way). Nonetheless, making these links is essential for our congregations even if the end applications look remarkably similar. First of all, this ensures that we make the right applications. We were careful in chapter 3 not to encourage making burnt offerings or building temples. We can only avoid such mistakes if we see careful lines to Christ as a key part of our application.

Second, it helps our hearers to see the shift that the changing of the covenants brings – in particular, the equipping that Christ Jesus now gives by His Spirit. For example, it would be easy in this passage to reduce 7:10 to a legalistic, graceless message: read the Bible more, do it, teach it. Those *are* the ultimate applications (see below) but

---

6. Arguably two sides of the same coin: one bringing us to God, the other bringing God to us.

we listen to them and respond to them living in the New Covenant, i.e. empowered by the Spirit whom the risen and ascended Jesus pours on the church.

From text to message
The passage can be preached as a whole or simply as one text (v. 10). I will suggest how these two sermons may differ below.

Getting the message clear: the theme
Ezra the priest is a man of the Law and favoured by God, so he returns to Jerusalem to instruct God's people.

Getting the message clear: the aim
See how God delights to bless those who love His word.

A way in
There are two possible ways to introduce the passage. One is historical. For example, it would be instructive to ask what the people needed. After all, they have finished the temple now and re-introduced the sacrificial system. But more is needed. In one sense there is a parallel here with the time of the Reformation. The structures seemed to be in place but the word of God was absent. Whilst serving a useful purpose (establishing some of the context), the preacher would have to work hard to avoid such an approach sounding very dull.

A second approach might introduce the applications up front by asking the question: what would a church look like where there was no teaching or commitment to the word of God? It would be chaotic at best, possibly heretical at worst. People would do their own thing without reference to others or to God. People would be in error because they 'do not know the Scriptures or the power of God'

(Matt. 22:29). Such an introduction could easily grab people's attention especially if it was framed in the context of 'this could be us'.

Ideas for application

- As noted above, application is best set in the context of seeing [Ezra → Jesus → Us] rather than simply [Ezra → Us]. Ezra's threefold devotion teaches us about Christ first, then what it means to follow Him and more particularly, the nature of the ministry for which He sets some apart.

- The 'Law of Moses' is the word that God speaks to His people revealing His nature and showing His people how to please Him and come close to Him. It is fulfilled, not primarily in New Testament commands, but in Christ Jesus, the word of God. However, it is the entire Bible which reveals the Son to us. In other words, it is appropriate to move from 'the Law' to 'the Bible' not because of a direct correlation but because of the way that Christ fulfils even the Law of Moses (see Matt. 5:17-20). Such a shift is important because we are not simply calling people to a new Law but to a person, whom the Law anticipates.

- The order of Ezra's commitment is significant. Personal devotion and obedience are prerequisites to teaching others (an idea picked up in various places, including Heb. 5:5-10).

- Ezra's trip and God's providential hand are linked to Ezra's love for the Law and his desire to teach it to others. This is a worthy cause and whilst we

can never presume on the sovereignty of God, it is
good to see what He loves to bless – here expressed
in a devotion to what He has said.

Suggestions for preaching

Sermon 1

A sermon on this whole section does most justice to the
way the text has been inspired. Our attention is then
drawn to the man of God in a broad sense rather than
focusing exclusively on his relationship to the Law. An
outline might run something like this:

- **The qualification of the man of God** (vv. 1-6).
  The lineage is important to validate Ezra's
  position. He is not an ordinary Israelite but comes
  from an extraordinary line. God is with him in
  extraordinary measure (v. 6).

- **The mission of the man of God** (vv. 7-10).
  Together with other Israelites Ezra comes to
  Jerusalem with God's blessing because he loves the
  Law, does the Law and wants to teach the Law.
  His mission is for others to share his devotion.

A key question with this kind of approach is to ask at
what stage the person of Christ is introduced. It doesn't
need to be at every stage (that might be rather clunky) but
He could be the answer to a question towards the end,
'Wouldn't it be great if we had an Ezra today?'

Sermon 2

A sermon on 7:10 would be neat and appropriate for a
number of occasions, *assuming that some of the context work
was still in place*. A descriptive set of headings would be:

- Ezra loved the Law
- Ezra did the Law
- Ezra taught the Law

However, such a sermon might be somewhat pedestrian. A better approach might be to do more context and Biblical theology up front and make the headings into applications.

- Will you love God's word?
- Will you do God's word?
- Will you teach God's word?

Suggestions for teaching

Questions to help understand the passage

1. When does this action take place (v. 1)? In Bible terms, what has happened since 6:22?

2. Why do we need to know Ezra's lineage? What does it tell us about him?

3. The text does not focus on Ezra's work as a priest offering sacrifices. What is its focus?

4. Why had God favoured Ezra? See verse 6 and also verse 9.

5. What does the passage tell us about Ezra's relationship to the Law?

Questions to help apply the passage

1. To whom does Ezra point? How? Think of examples.

2. In what way did God answer Jesus' requests and display His favour?

3. How does seeing Jesus as the fulfilment of Ezra help us (1) understand how we apply Ezra's love of the *Law* and (2) understand how we apply these truths to ourselves?

4. Read verse 10 again. Knowing that Jesus has come, how does this verse challenge us (1) as a church and (2) in supporting and praying for our leaders?

2. Another king, another letter (Ezra 7:11-28)

Introduction

We now arrive at Ezra's commissioning letter from the king which validates his work in Jerusalem. It is an important document, particularly when seen in the light of the opposition faced by the first exiles (chapter 4). In the letter the king also offers Ezra all kinds of financial help. This addition magnifies the letter's importance still further, given that these offers may well be questioned by Ezra's enemies and perhaps even forgotten by this or a future king.

However, as we have already seen, this letter was almost certainly a response to Ezra's own request (7:6) and we see similarities here to the events at the beginning of Ezra's companion book of Nehemiah (Neh. 2:8). The letter's preamble (v. 11) and conclusion (vv. 27-28) are written in Hebrew but the letter itself is recorded in Aramaic, probably because it was copied into the text from the court record. This switch of language validates the letter which contains (like Darius' letter in chapter 6) some surprising provisions. Once again we see the abundance of the providence of God.

Some critics make much of the apparent Jewish knowledge that seems to lie behind the letter. It should not be forgotten, however, that there was Jewish influence at court (through Artaxerxes' step-mother Esther and other officials like Nehemiah). Also, the letter might well have been written by Ezra himself for endorsement by the king. Such a process would not invalidate its nature or its content.

The focus of the letter is weighted towards the Law-keeping that Ezra is to establish, even though space is also given to the offering of sacrifices. This will be explored further in the explanation below.

Listening to the text
Context and structure
In broad terms, the passage contains a preamble and a conclusion (written in Hebrew) and a copy of the official letter (in Aramaic). The letter itself can be further sub-divided.

- Preamble: introducing the letter (v. 11)
- Letter (vv. 12-26)
    - ◇ Purpose of Ezra's mission (vv. 12-17)
    - ◇ Provision for Ezra's mission (vv. 18-24)
    - ◇ Propagation of Ezra's mission (vv. 25-26)
- Conclusion: Ezra's reflection on these events (vv. 27-28)

The letter is best seen as Artaxerxes' validation of Ezra's mission (hence the terminology above) rather than an initiative of the king to which Ezra responds. The letter lays out clearly the focus of Ezra's mission but this should not detract from seeing the extraordinary affirmation that this pagan king is giving to what is essentially a Jewish concern.

Working through the text

Preamble: introducing the letter (v. 11)
We learn that the letter which follows is a 'copy' which had been given to Ezra. This ensured that the original would

remain in the royal records but that Ezra also had written permission to enable him to fulfil his mission. The preamble (written by the author of Ezra rather than the king) confirms our understanding of the text: that although Ezra was a priest, his primary focus was ensuring that the Law was being treasured and followed.

Purpose of Ezra's mission (vv. 12-17)

We should not read anything into Artaxerxes' title ('king of kings'). It is simply an honorific title used in such documents. These first few verses establish the parameters of Ezra's mission. He is to collect any other exiles who wish to return (compare 1:3) and head back to Jerusalem. Ezra seems to be able to cast the net wide: 'any of the Israelites in my kingdom' could presumably include those resettled in the north together with other Jewish communities scattered in other places.

The king is keen to show that he not only endorses this trip but is behind it. 'You are sent by the king' seems to imply that the trip is entirely his initiative, but as we have already seen, this is unlikely to be the case. However, if Ezra is to be successful in the ancient autocracy of the Persian Empire he needs to ensure that what we know to be *his* mission is seen by the world as the *king's* mission.

Either way, the primary purpose of Ezra's trip is clear: he is to enquire about 'Judah and Jerusalem with regard to the Law of your God which is in your hand.' Such a primary purpose fits with the trajectory of the book. The temple has already been rebuilt and temple worship recommenced, but is God's Law being fully kept in the lives of God's people? The mission statement given in this letter clearly plays to Ezra's strengths (7:10). And as we read on we will see how much this mission is needed, for there are indeed deficiencies in the way the Law is being kept.

However, we must not separate this focus entirely from the operation of the temple and its sacrifices, for the daily and festival offerings are themselves part of the Law. It is not surprising therefore that the remainder of this short section (vv. 15-17) relates to the sacrifices to be offered in the temple. Such offerings were a key (perhaps *the* key) element of every near-eastern religion of the time and so it is not surprising that the king zooms in on this. This does not however detract from Ezra's main purpose which is also confirmed by the content of the rest of the book. If offerings and sacrifices are not accompanied by obedience to the rest of the Law then this is nothing more than empty religion.

Provision for Ezra's mission (vv. 18-24)

The next section contains some extraordinary statements. Ezra is given permission to use whatever is left over from the initial offerings in whatever way he sees fit. The qualification 'in accordance with the will of your God' does provide some restraint. Presumably the king means 'whatever else is consistent with the Law', which might, for example, include the ongoing work of offering sacrifices at the temple.

A careful reader will have noticed that all the stolen vessels had already been returned (1:7-11). It seems odd therefore that more 'articles' are identified here in verse 19. It seems best to see the items in verse 19 as part of the general provision of verse 20 where the king gives Ezra anything he may need in order to be able to operate the temple according to the Law.

This provision is made more specific in verses 21-24, both positively and negatively. First, positively, all the local treasurers (of the same area that Tattenai governed, see 5:3) are to provide the funding. Though within certain limits, this funding is incredibly generous (v. 22). In verse 24 we find a strong hint of the king's motivation in making sure Ezra's work is well resourced: 'Why should there be wrath against the realm of the king and his sons?' Ezra may have suggested this to the king or he may have thought it himself. The king's reasoning here is not unlike that of Darius in 6:10.

Secondly, negatively, the local authorities are to exempt the temple workers from any local taxation (v. 24). Their work must not be hindered in any way. The phrase 'taxes, tribute or duty' is the same one that appeared back in the letter to Artaxerxes recorded in chapter 4.

Propagation of Ezra's mission (vv. 25-26)

Finally, Ezra is tasked with making sure his review of the Law (v. 14) goes beyond mere enquiry ('how are things going?') to ensuring that the Law is being kept. Ezra is to appoint fellow Law-experts to teach alongside him. Moreover, there are to be severe punishments for those who do not obey (v. 26).

This last sentence perplexes some readers. Does the pagan Persian king really want to enforce Jewish law? Would it not be better for him to be enforcing Persian law instead? There is probably no need to draw so sharp a distinction. In exile keeping the Jewish law was for the most part consistent with local rule. Even though Israel was constituted as a theocracy, most of their laws enabled them to thrive under occupation or foreign rule (see for example, God's letter to the exiles in Jer. 29). No doubt a simple reading of the Law (or an explanation of it by Ezra) would have been enough

to show the king how good it would be for the entire nation
for God's Law to be enforced.

Moreover, it was much more likely that Jewish people
could be persuaded to keep Jewish law rather than having
the Persian system imposed upon them. In other words,
Artaxerxes' willingness to get behind Ezra and his mission
was probably nothing less than political expediency on his
part, good though it was for the Lord's people. Very often
God's people benefit from events and circumstances which
are carried out for the most selfish of motives.

Conclusion: reflection on the events (vv. 27-28)

The last two verses of our section are Ezra's reflection on
the events that led to the king's letter being written. They
bring together key ideas. First, Ezra is full of praise to
God for the way that He has moved the king (cf. 1:1) to
endorse Ezra's mission. This mission will bring 'honour to
the house of the Lord'. This does not indicate a change in
Ezra's main purpose, which is establishing the Law; rather
it is a shorthand way of describing that the Law is to be
integrated back into the whole of Jewish life which has its
focus in the temple worship.

Ezra is clear that the good hand of God has now given
him standing before 'the king and his advisors and all the
king's powerful officials' – the addition of the adjective
'powerful' underlining the extraordinary nature of what
God has done. Finally, Ezra returns to a familiar theme
– it is this same sovereign rule of God that has given him
the courage to gather leaders and set off back to Jerusalem.

Connection with chapter 4

It is worth pausing and asking about this passage's links to chapter 4. There we saw how Rehum and Shimshai wrote to this same king urging him to stop the work that was going on in Jerusalem (4:8-23), a request which was granted freely (4:21). How are we to reconcile this with the events of chapter 7?

There are two possible answers.[7] The first is found in the difference in character between the two projects. The project in view in chapter 4 is clearly a building project: 'they are restoring the walls and repairing the foundations' (4:12). Ezra's mission is altogether different. His is a theological project rather than a civil engineering one. Artaxerxes would not be threatened by law-keeping citizens in the same way he might by those who were rebuilding their city.

This solution doesn't fully answer the question, however, for Artaxerxes *does* later endorse rebuilding the city walls (see Neh. 1-2). We therefore need to look for a further answer and find one in the time difference between the king's contrasting responses. There is no indication in chapter 4 as to exactly when Artaxerxes wrote his negative letter. The events of that chapter are simply described as occurring 'in the days of Artaxerxes' (4:7), whereas 7:9 (and Neh. 1:1) give us clear date markers for his positive responses.

It is not unreasonable therefore to assume that the events of chapter 4 took place early in the king's reign with the turnaround in Ezra and Nehemiah taking place later

---

7. This is a question rarely tackled by commentaries, but a thinking reader or sermon-listener might consider it a fair question.

on. If this were indeed the case, it would make the change God wrought in Artaxerxes even more remarkable.

From text to message

This passage confirms the themes we have already seen emerging in the second part of Ezra. We now have confirmed through an official record the way that God has been preparing the king to endorse Ezra's mission. There are therefore key lessons here about the way God works in history.

Getting the message clear: the theme

King Artaxerxes gets fully behind Ezra's mission to ensure Israel keeps the Law of Moses.

Getting the message clear: the aim

God uses all means to back His servants including the most surprising ones. We need to be careful not to use the passage to preach absolutes from what is an example. The story is descriptive and as such it neither requires God always to act in this way nor limits Him to doing only this. The encouragement for us today is to see the way God is at work behind the scenes.

A way in

There are lots of examples from history of how secular rulers have supported gospel initiatives in the most surprising ways. The preacher could introduce these but needs to do so with care because many Christians will feel nostalgic for a bygone age where such support from the state was the norm. Stories like these are only useful if we can avoid the implication that such help is normal and therefore a right for us in any age.

A better way to start this sermon might be to introduce the problem the passage addresses, namely, how on earth is Ezra going to fulfil his mission? We need to feel the impossibility of the task before him. He is living in an autocratic secular state and he wants to introduce the Law of Moses into a Persian outpost. What king would be behind such a plan and how could Ezra ever hope to avoid the opposition we read of in chapter 4? Laying out all these practical difficulties sets the scene for the main teaching points and also goes with the thrust of the text. It is therefore better in almost every way than introducing non-typical examples of secular support.

Ideas for application

- Ezra gets the secular endorsement he needs to carry out his project. He cannot presume on this, but when it comes he recognises God's good hand behind it and it fills him with joy.

- As in other sections of Ezra there are lessons about the surprising way God moves the hearts of secular rulers to get behind His work.

- It may be tempting to draw conclusions about the relationships between church and state, for example on whether ministers of churches should be exempt from tax (7:24) or whether the crown should impose penalties on those who break church rules (7:26) as happened with blasphemy laws. This is surely reading too much into the text. These are examples of God's providence rather than inviolable rights or privileges which should be applied in every age.

- Ezra recognises that God's sovereignty not only moves the king, it also provides the courage that Ezra himself needs to pursue the calling he has been given.

- Even though the focus is on Ezra in the passage, he collects around him people who will support him (v. 28), an action which opens up some interesting lines of application.

Suggestions for preaching

Sermon 1
It is best to keep the letter and Ezra's theological reflections (in vv. 27-28) together. In essence, the reflections contain the teaching points and the letter the illustrations of them. All of this is expressed in the context of Ezra's mission and answers the question 'How will this work get done?' In this case the controlling idea is God's sovereign hand.

God's mission is fulfilled through:

- **His providential rule of world events.** This point would pick up on the extraordinary statements of the letter, including provision and protection. All this happens, whether it is recognised or not, because God has 'extended his good favour to' Ezra and his plans.

- **His gracious provision of godly leaders.** This second point picks up on Ezra himself and his own recognition that God's hand has been upon him. This is not simply a backward- looking concept because Ezra recognises that God's continued overruling is needed for him to fulfil his mission.

Sermons 2 and 3

A second approach would be to teach the conclusion in verses 27-28 separately from the letter. This would deal well with the theological reflections that Ezra summarises but might leave the letter feeling disconnected from its context. With this approach, sermon 2 might work through the letter showing how it reveals God's sovereign hand and then sermon 3 would pick up on the reflections separately, showing that God is worth praising because:

- He works through pagan rulers to achieve His purposes
- He gives courage to His leaders to pursue His mission
- He gathers His people together to fulfil His plans

All of this should lead to praise (v. 27), a slightly different emphasis from the whole chapter (where the focus is more on how the mission will be completed).

As with other parts of Ezra, these sermons need to be connected appropriately and carefully to the work of Christ. The best way to do this is to reflect on the mission that Ezra has been given and the way God works all things out in order to achieve His purposes.

Suggestions for teaching

Questions to help understand the passage

1. Read through Artaxerxes' letter of commendation again. Note all the surprising ways God is at work behind the scenes.

2. What seems to be the main reason behind Ezra's mission? How do we know?

3. Why was such a letter necessary for Ezra?

4. According to Ezra's own reflections in verses 27-28, in what two ways has God been at work?

5. Why does Ezra need courage for the future?

6. What response does God's working stir in Ezra (v. 27)?

Questions to help apply the passage

1. What does this passage teach us about what we can expect in our interactions with the world?

2. Why should we be careful about drawing direct comparisons with our situation today?

3. Why doesn't Ezra act alone and what can we learn from the fact that he gathers people around him?

4. Think about the life, death and resurrection of Christ. How were the factors which enabled Ezra's mission to be accomplished at work in Christ's mission?

5. Think about your own church situation. How does reading and understanding this passage change the way you (1) think and (2) act?

3. Home again (Ezra 8:1-36)

Introduction

Chapter 8 is a reasonably long section that deals with the practical aspects of the journey to Jerusalem. Like chapter 2 it includes a list of those returning. The chapter is best studied as a single unit as each section within it (see below) follows on seamlessly from the previous one. One significant problem with the return was that initially the returning group included no Levites (v. 15). Levites were needed to maintain the work of the temple (v. 17). Throughout the chapter there is a continued emphasis on the sovereignty of God both in the journey itself (v. 31) and also in the provision of the Levites (v. 18). The language of the passage ('the gracious hand of our God was on us' – v. 18) conveys continuity with the previous section (compare 7:28).

This second return to Jerusalem is nothing like the size of the first. In all, the list in chapter 8 names 1,496 men to whom 258 Levites and temple servants are later added (vv. 18-20). Even allowing for women and children this return could not have exceeded eight thousand compared to the fifty thousand plus who returned the first time around. Some commentators think that the list given here may be incomplete; the fact that there are twelve subtotals listed may be symbolic rather than a snapshot of a greater whole. But there is no reason to suppose this is the case and the precise nature of the figures in the list hints at completeness rather than symbolism.

Moreover, we need to remember that the second return (unlike the first) is focused around one individual, Ezra, and the mission he is given to complete: to establish the Law of Moses amongst the people of God. The preacher or teacher needs to keep this mission in mind when expounding this passage.

Listening to the text

Context and structure

Chapter 8 picks up on some details that we first saw in the introduction to the second part of Ezra in chapter 7 – most noticeably that 'Some of the Israelites, including priests, Levites, singers, gatekeepers and temple servants, also came up to Jerusalem in the seventh year of King Artaxerxes' (7:7). However, this summary sentence hides a significant problem that is addressed in this chapter: when Ezra came to survey the volunteers who were returning, he found no Levites (v. 15). There is also an additional issue to address. The exiles will have a large quantity of valuables with them – some provided by the king and some given voluntarily by other Israelites. Ezra must work out how to transport these safely: no easy task over a long desert journey.

The text splits up neatly into five sections, all to do with the journey:

- The travellers (vv. 1-14)

- Issue #1: Finding Levites (vv. 15-20)

- Issue #2: Travelling protection (vv. 21-30)

- The journey (vv. 31-32)

- The arrival (vv. 33-36)

Working through the text

The travellers (vv. 1-14)

The list of returnees shares some similarities with chapter 2 but the introduction identifies it as being a personal record rather than an official one. The men listed are those 'who came up with me' – i.e. those who shared in Ezra's mission. Significantly, the list starts with two fellow priests named Gershom and Daniel and another man, a direct descendant of David called Hattush. Nothing more is heard of these characters but their inclusion mirrors the first section of the book where again, a priest, Joshua, and a descendant of David, Zerubbabel, were main characters.

The list then continues with twelve further groups. The number may be significant, seeking to represent the entirety of the nation (see notes on 2:2). Certainly, in this second section of the book the language of nationhood and Israel is prominent (see for example, 9:1) and there seems an implicit assumption that those who have returned to Jerusalem are now the sole representatives of the chosen people.

All the family names in the list also appear in chapter 2 although not all the family names in chapter 2 appear here, again indicating the smallness of this company of men compared to the initial group. As with chapter 2, a technical commentary will give some insight into particular names but unlike the earlier list there seems to be no particular point being made here about groups or temple workers. Clearly, those returning first time around did not represent the entirety of families or clans. Kidner points out that this increases our sense of marvel at those who returned first time around.[8]

One phrase stands out as being unusual: 'of the descendants of Adonikam, *the last ones*, whose names were Eliphelet, Jeuel and Shemaiah; and with them 60 men' (v. 13). In what sense were these the last ones? Most probably this phrase

---

tells us that these descendants were the last of that family in Babylon.[9] If so, then the strong implication is that each of the other eleven families had relatives who were still left behind. Just as we are to marvel at those who first returned, we are also to marvel at this second group who signed up for Ezra's mission.

Issue #1: Finding Levites (vv. 15-20)

Two issues now present themselves. First, when Ezra assembled those who were willing to accompany him he discovered a lack of Levites (v. 15). The text implies that he was actively searching for them rather than that he simply 'noticed' there were none. Why, however, did Ezra need Levites if his mission was to ensure that the Law was followed?

We have already seen that the temple operation was critical to the full keeping of the Law of Moses. The Levites served at the temple as 'attendants' (v. 17). Their original function was to transport the Tabernacle and all its associated paraphernalia (see Num. 3-4); this function was later extended to protecting the Tabernacle (Num. 18). Levites appear from time to time in the rest of the Old Testament histories, for example as temple musicians.[10] Their role in carrying the holy objects is almost certainly what is being picked up here; for, as we shall see, there is a huge amount of money and valuables to transport to Jerusalem.

The Levites had also been symbolically given to God as a substitute for the first born (see Num. 3:11-12). To

---

9. Williamson, p. 108.

10. For a more detailed survey, see *The New Bible Dictionary*, 3rd Edition (Leicester, UK: IVP, 1996), p. 956.

return to Jerusalem without any Levites would be to dis-
regard the way God had previously redeemed His people;
this would be out of line with the strong Exodus echoes
in the book.

Ezra therefore summons nine leaders and two 'men of
learning', an otherwise unknown phrase.[11] These men will
serve as intermediaries with 'Iddo, the leader in Casiphia.'
It is not clear what significance we should attach to this
place, other than it seems to have been the place where
temple servants were operating (v. 17), perhaps in a kind
of make-shift temple.

The appeal is successful, producing thirty-eight Levites
and a further two hundred and twenty temple servants (a
role that is further explained for us with reference to the
reforming work of David, see v. 20). There are some textual
questions over the family names[12], but the main point is
clear: even the provision of this small number of Levites
and their assistants is down to 'the gracious hand of our
God' (v. 18).

Issue #2: Travelling protection (vv. 21-30)

The second issue facing Ezra is more prosaic but not
unconnected. We have already seen that the exiles will be
returning with a large quantity of valuables. The king has
promised funding (7:15) and also encouraged others to
support the cause (7:16). We are told the exact amounts: 650
talents of silver, plus a further 100 talents of silver articles;
100 talents of gold and twenty golden bowls (together with

---

11. It does appear in a different context in Job 42:2.

12. Mahli (v. 18) was a grandson of Levi (son of Merari). It is unclear
why Hashabiah and Jeshaiah and their twenty compatriots are listed
separately as sons of Merari.

their value of 1,000 darics), and 'two fine articles of polished bronze' (v. 27). This extraordinary collection represents over twenty-five tonnes of silver and over eight kilos of gold. No wonder Ezra is nervous. Unlike the first return, the numbers of exiles may well not be large enough to dissuade attackers and so Ezra recognises that the travelling company might be at risk from the ancient equivalent of highwaymen.

Ezra is ashamed to ask the king to provide him with armed protection on the journey because he has told the king, 'The gracious hand of our God is on everyone who looks to him, but his great anger is against all who forsake him' (v. 22). Ezra also testified to this belief that God's hand and favour were upon him in 7:27-28, but does he really believe it? The text suggests that he does, though it also suggests that Ezra is humble enough not to presume on God. Why else would Ezra proclaim a fast (mentioned twice, see v. 21 and v. 23) and a prayer time to accompany it?

In the Old Testament fasting is associated with repentance rather than decision-making and that is clearly the case here. The fast was so that 'we might humble ourselves' (v. 21). In other words, Ezra realises that God responds sovereignly to those who are right before Him. Ezra does not presume on the protection he has told the king he will enjoy.

In an almost throwaway line, Ezra tells us the good news. 'He answered our prayer' (v. 23). This does not seem to be a direct 'spoken' answer but rather this is Ezra's reflection as he looks back on the journey after they have arrived safely in Jerusalem (v. 32); he recognises that God did indeed do what the people asked of Him.

The careful counting of all the treasure (vv. 24-30) is a practical necessity – Ezra is, after all, a servant of the king who has provided much of it. But there is a theological point being made here also. The 'articles are consecrated to the LORD' – that is, they are set apart for Him and are to be used in His temple. The loose cash is a 'freewill offering to the LORD', so great care must be taken over it too. It is to be guarded 'carefully' until it can be counted out in the temple (v. 29, compare v. 33). This sacrificial language reinforces how important it is that the priests and Levites are keeping a close check on all these valuables.

The journey (vv. 31-32)

Once these two problems are addressed and resolved, the journey itself is described in very brief terms. We have already been told its duration (7:9). Now we are told that the start was delayed by twelve days (compare 7:9 with v. 31), presumably to resolve the Levitical issue. Just as Ezra had promised the king, 'the hand of our God was on us, and he protected us from enemies and bandits along the way.'

The arrival (v. 33-36)

The final section of this passage describes the arrival in Jerusalem. After a brief rest (v. 32) the treasure is counted out into the hands of priests and Levites who were already present in Jerusalem. These include some familiar names (both Eleazar and Phinehas are ancient High Priestly names). Most significantly, 'everything was accounted for by number and weight' (v. 34).

The last two verses of our passage switch away from the first-person description we have enjoyed so far. This is no longer Ezra speaking but a third person describing the sacrifices offered. They are twice described as burnt offerings (at the beginning and end of the verse) though the actual sacrifices themselves do not fit the pattern laid out in Leviticus 1. This is probably because these offerings represented a one-off sacrifice rather than being part of the established routine of the temple. With the exception of the male lambs, each sacrifice is divisible by twelve, once again showing us that these offerings are being made 'for all Israel.'

The final piece of the jigsaw is described in verse 36 as the letter of chapter 7 ('the king's orders') is delivered to all the local officials. Ezra is home and his mission is ready to begin.

From text to message

This is one of the more difficult passages within Ezra to preach and teach. This is because although the theme is reasonably clear (we see a continued emphasis in the text on 'the hand of God on us'), the outworking of this providence is in purely practical terms – the abundance of the offerings, the provision of Levites and the safe journeying.

These provisions are appropriate to the context of the covenant of that time in which God had promised His faithful servants prosperity if they were faithful to Him (see for example, Deut. 28:1-14). However, we do not live under the covenant of Moses and failing to recognise this fact will lead us to the wrong applications and even to a kind of 'prosperity now' gospel, something which God does not promise us.

At best, then, the examples in the passage are illustrations of God's goodness to His people but they cannot be claimed or presumed upon this side of Calvary. The disconnection makes preaching the passage less than straightforward. However, James Hamilton is surely right to say that though we cannot promise that God will bless us in these precise ways, 'I can promise you that if you will do what Ezra does, if you will turn from your sin and seek the Lord in the person of the Lord Jesus Christ, you will experience the good hand of God on your life.'[13] The preacher or teacher will have to take care to define precisely how the Bible understands this 'good' that God promises to believers now.

This line of understanding also helps us in our Christological thinking. Ezra knows God's blessing because of his repentance (indicated by the fasting). We rely on Christ who never needed to fast and we seek God's forgiveness in His name and so we enjoy great blessing for good through Him.

Getting the message clear: the theme
God's good hand on humble Ezra means that all the exiles and their offerings arrive safely in Jerusalem ready to embark on Ezra's mission.

Getting the message clear: the aim
The text deliberately points us towards the sovereign hand of God just as it has in the two previous sections. God's providence is shown here in the precise practical outcomes noted above and we need to use these as illustrations of God's goodness rather than promises to be claimed or presumed upon.

A way in
A good approach here would be to ask what blessing really looks like for Christians. I like to introduce this at the start of the sermon because getting this right at the

---

13. Hamilton, J., *Christ-centred exposition, Ezra and Nehemiah* (Nashville, USA: Holman Reference, 2014), p. 77.

beginning avoids lots of dead ends or listeners joining dots that are never meant to be joined. For example, a general introduction about how God blesses us might wrongly lead people to expect the same tangible blessings that Ezra enjoyed. If the preacher only corrects this assumption right at the end of the talk, then hearers might well leave feeling disappointed rather than elated.

A better opening would show how the ways in which God blesses us today in Christ are more significant and lasting than the physical blessings of the Old Covenant. This will set the tone for the sermon and hearers will be able to listen to the story thinking, 'that's a great illustration, but God promises me something even better.'

Ideas for application

- God's hand is on His people for good. This sovereign purpose is seen in the provision of those who will travel with Ezra and share his mission (v. 28), the Levites who are needed for the journey and beyond (v. 18), the abundant treasures provided by the king and others, and the safe travelling to Jerusalem.

- There is a human side to the sovereignty of God which is evidenced in the way Ezra and his colleagues humble themselves before God (v. 21).

- The blessings Christians enjoy are earned for us by Christ and are therefore complete and secure. We do not have the kind of relationship with God where He blesses our every good deed and curses our every bad one. That was the nature, in some respects, of the Old Covenant. Rather, it is Christ who has perfectly kept the Law for us and so earned and guaranteed the blessings that we now enjoy in Him.

- The blessings we enjoy in Christ (see for example, Eph. 1) are *better* than the old physical blessings of the Mosaic covenant, for they are both *spiritual* and *eternal*. Preachers and teachers should note that this is a key idea to convey; hearers find it hard to see how, say, *adoption* is better in every way than money in the bank or a healthy life.

Suggestions for preaching

Sermon 1: a narrative sermon structure

As with all such passages it is always possible to 're-tell' the story before drawing lines of application. I generally avoid doing this unless the passage absolutely demands it. Bible stories are generally well-told and well-crafted and simply reading them aloud is often sufficient. However, for this section I have included a narrative outline by way of illustration. This one comes from Hamilton.[14]

- Those who returned with Ezra (vv. 1-14)
- Lacking Levites (vv. 15-20)
- Preparation: Fasting and Funding (vv. 21-30)
- Safe Passage, Silver and Sacrifices (vv. 31-36)

The preacher would have to be careful not to be too pedestrian. Such headings can rob a colourful and interesting passage of some of its drama. If the sermon is following the narrative structure of this passage, a better way in would probably be to convey something of the

---

14. Hamilton, p. 70.

anticipation of a journey and the things that need to be considered before setting off. Then the application and lines to Christ would come at the end. This narrative approach is likely to be unsuitable if preaching time is short.

Sermon 2: *applicatory sermon structure*

For a vivid story like this one which 'tells itself' it is always a good plan to introduce the application as soon as possible and then let it flow throughout the sermon. This makes more natural use of the narrative structure that is present in the text. In this case, a good introduction can introduce the shift from Old Testament blessing to New Testament blessing (and how we receive this in Christ), as outlined above. The story then serves to illustrate the *nature* of this blessing.

- **God's sovereign blessing gathers people together for mission.** This point picks up on the last verse of the previous section and encourages us to marvel at the way this list of exiles is brought together for Ezra's mission.

- **God's sovereign blessing equips us for service.** This point is based on the provision of Levites for service. Their service was particular; ours is different, but no less important; we, like the Levites, are consecrated for God's service.

- **God's sovereign blessing brings us great riches.** The extraordinary size of the collection of gold, silver and articles for worship needs to be picked up here. There is an abundance in God's provision (compare chapter 1).

- **God's sovereign blessing protects us on our journey.** The safety that the Israelites enjoy is a reflection of the safety we enjoy as we travel to the New Jerusalem.

Key to this approach is seeing that the humble repentance we observe in Ezra (v. 21) is what joins us to the perfect servant Jesus Christ. We cannot enjoy these blessings without Him or without true repentance.

Suggestions for teaching

Questions to help understand the passage

1. What do we discover about those who returned (read from 7:28 and on into 8:15)?

2. Why does the absence of Levites matter? Check verse 17 and verse 28 for an answer.

3. How, practically, does Ezra go about finding Levites? What is the spiritual lesson he learns (v. 18)?

4. Why does Ezra fear for the journey? What has he said to the king about it?

5. Why does he fast and pray before he sets off?

6. What are we to think of the *amount* of treasure that is taken with Ezra and the others?

7. What happens on the journey?

8. What happens after the journey?

Questions to help apply the passage

1. Ezra enjoys the blessings that come from following God. Should we expect the same blessings? Why or why not?

2. What kinds of blessings does the New Testament promise us?

3. Why are these better than the blessings Ezra receives?

4. How is Ezra's attitude (v. 21) key to our understanding of blessings?

5. How do the details of the story shed light on the nature of the blessings we receive today?

4. Disobedience and confession (Ezra 9:1-15)

Introduction

This second half of Ezra now begins to move towards a sharp conclusion as we learn of a pressing issue that has arisen in the intervening years between chapters 1-6 and chapter 7 onwards: that of intermarriage. First, in chapter 9 Ezra leads the people in a corporate response to the issue. Then in chapter 10 we discover what is to be done in practical terms to deal with this sin.

These two chapters are tricky for two reasons: first, the desire to avoid intermarriage looks remarkably like modern day ethnic cleansing or racism. We need to help hearers see that this intermarriage is Mosaic Law-breaking and why it is so dangerous. Second, once we have established that fact, there remain difficulties with application (these will arise primarily in preaching chapter 10). For example, should Christians who are married to unbelievers divorce their spouses? Would that be the correct contemporary application of this passage? At one level, that seems to be what the text might suggest. As we shall see, however, such a conclusion would represent a failure to see how the whole Bible fits together and a failure to see how lines of application work.

Although most modern translations give our section in chapter 9 the heading 'Ezra's prayer about intermarriage' or something similar, the prayer is actually a response to the circumstances which are uncovered in the first few verses. We need to be careful not to make this simply a teaching section about prayer (though it is not less than that). To do so would be to rip the prayer out of its historical context.

Listening to the text

Context and structure

We are not told at this stage how long it took for these
events to take place. 'After these things had been done'
(v. 1) is a vague introduction. Later, in chapter 10 there
is a strong inference that several months had passed (the
assembly which is called immediately after Ezra's prayer
takes place some three and half months after Ezra's first
arrival in Jerusalem: see 10:9). The text itself falls into
three sections with most space being given to the third:

- Problem (vv. 1-2)

- Pause (vv. 3-4)

- Prayer (vv. 5-15)

The prayer itself has four clear sections. Carson outlines
the prayer in these terms:

- What brought about exile (vv. 6-7)

- The return is all of grace (vv. 8-9)

- In the light of this, intermarriage is defiant (vv. 10-12)

- Sin is complex and corrosive (vv. 13-15)[15]

With a little amendment, this could be a useful sermon
outline (see below).

I have used the same divisions, but with slightly different
headings, namely:

- Historic assessment (vv. 6-7)

- Acknowledgement of grace (vv. 8-9)

---

15. Carson, D. A., *For the love of God, volume 2* (Wheaton, USA: Crossway Books, 1998), entry for January 9.

- Current assessment (vv. 10-12)
- Continuing need of grace (vv. 13-15)

I will address the particular presenting sin of intermarriage more fully in chapter 10 as it is there that it is finally dealt with.

Working through the text
Problem (vv. 1-2)

First, we (and Ezra himself) are introduced to the problem by 'the leaders' – presumably the godly leaders who have resisted this particular temptation (cf. v. 2b). It is important to see this conversation as an indication of the crisis which, under God, Ezra has returned to address. We should recall that we established the overall theme of the book as being 'The Lord providentially restores His people so that they can worship and honour Him.' At the heart of the honour the Lord deserves is obedience to His word in the Law of Moses.

When Ezra was introduced it was as one well-versed in the Law and he was commissioned by the king to ensure that the Law was being observed. It is no surprise, therefore, to discover that the flash-point of Ezra's ministry is to do with a failure to keep this Law, in particular the sin of intermarriage.

The leaders' complaint to Ezra is clear: certain people have not 'kept themselves separate from the neighbouring people with their detestable practices.' More specifically, they have taken foreign women and either married them themselves or given them as wives to their sons. As a result they have 'mingled the holy race with the peoples around them.' Worse still, the 'leaders and officials have led the way in this unfaithfulness.' This is a top-down sin.

This problem was not widespread, as we will see in chapter 10. For a start there are some leaders (those who come to Ezra) who have not taken part in this sin. Nevertheless, the way the objection is phrased (v. 1) and the way that Ezra responds demonstrates that there is a corporate nature to this sin that affects the whole nation.

There is no Law that prohibits all intermarriage. Indeed, some of the most well-known women of the Old Testament are Gentiles who have married into the people of Israel (e.g. Moses' wife, Zipporah and Boaz' wife, Ruth). However, we should not confuse these Gentile converts (who embraced the Jewish faith) with the wives referred to in Ezra 9. The reference to the 'detestable practices' allows for no such sentimentality. Perhaps we should think instead of Solomon's wives who turned his heart away from the Lord (1 Kings 11:1-6) or even Jezebel (1 Kings 16:31). These kings were seriously compromised by their wives' idolatry and their spiritual downfall contributed to Israel being sent into exile in the first place (a fact which is reflected in Ezra's prayer).

With the exception of intermarriage that was accompanied by conversion, the Law's verdict on the practice was very negative: Exodus 34:16 contains a strong implication that intermarriage is prohibited; Deuteronomy 7:3 is more explicit (though it is stated in the context of conquest). The list of nations in Deuteronomy 7 bears a remarkable resemblance to that in Ezra 9. (See notes on vv. 11-12 for further comment on the Law and how it is broken by intermarriage.)

Why is this sin so serious? It is called 'unfaithfulness' by the leaders and Ezra's response does nothing to diminish the implications of this language. It is important to see this breach in the light of the covenant and the promises that God had made to Israel. Intermarriage (unless accompanied by conversion, an exception for which the Law provided) would always lead Israel astray, 'for they will turn your children away from following me to serve other gods, and the Lord's anger will burn against you and quickly destroy you' (Deut. 7:4). What is at stake here is not *racial* purity but *spiritual* purity and – finally – faithfulness to the covenant. No wonder then that the same theme of unfaithfulness is picked up by Malachi (e.g. Mal. 2:10-12), a prophet contemporary to the time of Ezra.

A good sermon or Bible study will establish from the outset the precise nature of the unfaithfulness in view here, thereby helping to head off questions (spoken or otherwise) about racism or ethnic cleansing. Nothing less than the spiritual existence of the nation is at stake.

Pause (vv. 3-4)

Whilst it is tempting to launch straight into the prayer, it is worth reflecting first on verses 3-4. It is quite possible to get a sense of how Ezra feels about the sin from the words of his prayer but this initial response – essentially one of stunned silence mingled with grief – is portrayed very powerfully. There are several elements to his response.

First, tearing of clothes indicated deep distress (see for example 2 Sam. 13:19). Ezra is very upset by what he has learnt. The pulling of hair and beard indicates grief, a slightly different emotion. He then 'sat down appalled' – almost as though the weight of what he had heard kept him from bearing his own weight. He then spends a day in silence (v. 4b) accompanied by others who shared his grief.

It must surely have been comforting to Ezra to know he was not alone in his grief though it seems to have taken someone with Ezra's stature (and possibly his authority) to actually bring about change. However, the main point of this little section is to show how upset Ezra was by this sin (and its possible ramifications for the nation). As such, it is instructive to us. We tend to be very intellectual about sin, rarely 'feeling' its weight (compare 2 Cor. 11:29 where Paul 'inwardly burn[s]').

Prayer (vv. 5-15)

Ezra's response is most obviously seen in his prayer. Ezra's prayer is largely formed as a prayer on behalf of the whole nation. It is a comprehensive, corporate response to what is – essentially – a comprehensive, corporate problem. Tempting as it is to see in Ezra's response a model for *praying*, it is more instructive to see in his prayer an appropriate response to *sin* which will then in turn instruct our own praying. Good pray-ers are first and foremost those who have grasped the fundamentals of the faith, including the seriousness of sin, the nature of God and what He has done in the gospel.

Ezra's prayer is both personal ('O my God, I am ashamed…' v. 6) and corporate ('the LORD our God has been gracious in leaving us…' v. 8). However, this almost certainly reflects the exact nature of Ezra's role and mission rather than being a prescription for the form of every prayer that should be offered by every Christian. Nevertheless, there is something here for us to learn about how the gathered people of God pray *together*.

Historic assessment (v. 6-7) = what we were
Ezra's prayer begins with what we might term 'historic' confession. He recognises that at this key moment in Israel's history he must acknowledge what has got them to this point. The nation is past its glory and the people have been subjected to 'the sword and captivity, to pillage

and humiliation at the hand of foreign kings.' Despite their
return to Jerusalem this ongoing captivity continues – 'as
it is today' (v. 7). In other words, captivity for Israel is not
simply a geographic issue: rather, they are still not their
own masters even though they have been allowed to return
to the capital, build the city and re-establish the Law. Ezra
begins by outlining what the nation was and still is now.

This realistic view of the current situation is important.
Ezra's words are not a confession as we might understand
one: at no point does Ezra pray for forgiveness. However,
his prayer does identify that it is the sin of the nation that
has brought it to its knees and to its current plight. He is
honest about this and this acknowledgement of failure at
the beginning of the prayer reflects the humility and reality
with which any believer needs to approach God.

Ezra's prayer is also colourful. He uses language and
phrases that invoke the senses – both the metaphors he
uses ('higher than our heads' and 'guilt has reached to the
heavens') paint a picture of the enormity of the sin. This
will show the grace which is outlined in the next section to
be even more extraordinary. The punishment that has come
upon the people of God (and still to an extent remains) is
also painted with a dramatic palette of vocabulary (v. 7).

Acknowledgement of grace (vv. 8-9) = what God has done
Ezra now turns to outline what God has done in gracious
response to this desperate situation. Ezra draws a contrast
('But now') and then proceeds to outline the grace of God.
Again, the language is beautiful in the way it portrays the
precise nature of what God has done. Ezra's choice of
words could have been much more functional; he could
have just said, 'God brought us back, He gave us a temple.'

Instead, the vocabulary he chooses is both more emotive and also more profoundly theological.

For example, Ezra sees in Israel's return a doctrine of the 'remnant' (v. 8, v. 13 and v. 15); the Lord has given 'a firm place in his sanctuary' (which conveys so much more than just, 'the temple was rebuilt'); and the poetic phrasing of verse 8b ('our God gives light to our eyes and a little relief in our bondage'). Ezra again manages to match beauty with realism in his assessment.

Verse 9 describes four ways this gracious faithfulness can be seen:

- God has not deserted His people
- God has providentially worked through the 'kings of Persia'
- God has given life so that the people could rebuild the temple
- God has given a 'wall of protection in Judah and Jerusalem.'[16]

This reflection on God's grace is important for Ezra. It stands in contrast to the people's sinfulness, and as we see both their sin and God's grace clearly, there is no doubt that the restoration the people have enjoyed is only and all of God's initiative. Moreover, it is no small thing that God has done as this four-fold explanation makes clear.

Current assessment (v. 10-12) = what we are now
This, however, is not the end of the story. Just as God's grace was introduced with a 'But now' in verse 8, so this next

---

16. The mind is inevitably drawn to the wall-building exploits of Nehemiah. However, not only does this project come later in our timeline, but Ezra is clearly speaking metaphorically as there was never any wall around Judah.

section is introduced in the same way. Ezra goes on to reflect on what he has now learnt about their current situation. Remembering God's grace to them in the restoration of the temple (vv. 8-9) might have led him immediately to rejoicing and praise but, given the news he has just received, instead Ezra admits further failure. For though God has re-established worship at the temple (giving them a 'firm place in the sanctuary' v. 8), the people's obedience to God's commands has not matched this restoration.

Further disobedience has followed, ironically of the very same type that took them into exile in the first place. Ezra then states the commands that have been violated by using a quotation – this is not a direct quotation from any Law or prophet but is rather 'a conglomeration of expressions borrowed from various parts of Scripture'[17] including Deuteronomy 4:5, Leviticus 18:25, Lamentations 1:17, 2 Kings 21:16, Isaiah 1:19 and more. 'The texts are not literally cited, but the essentials of the thought pattern are there.'[18]

There is an interesting logic to Ezra's praying, for whilst believers are not to dwell on their past in unhelpful ways, remembering what we once were has a number of benefits. It is key to appreciating the vastness of the grace of God and it also helps us to be honest about our likely temptations. It might have helped Israel avoid returning to her besetting sins.

Continuing need of grace (vv. 13-15) = what they now deserve
Ezra ends his prayer of confession in a surprising way. Once again, he doesn't overtly ask for forgiveness but instead he outlines what he knows of the justice and mercy of God. He knows the people deserve punishment. He knows too

---

17. Fensham, p. 131.
18. Fensham, p. 131.

that God has acted towards them with mercy both in the past and – to a certain extent – in the present. As Ezra ends his prayer, he leaves with God this tension between His justice and His mercy.

When it comes to justice, 'What has happened to us is a result of our evil deeds' (v. 13) and 'Would you not be angry enough with us to destroy us, leaving us no remnant or survivor?' (v. 14). But God's justice has been tempered with mercy, a fact Ezra reflects on both in the past ('you have punished us less than our sins have deserved') and in the present ('we are left this day as a remnant').

One of the interesting things about this prayer is the way that Ezra does not do what we would exactly expect in a prayer of confession (though that is what it is – see 10:1). Rather, this is the prayer of a man who is throwing himself entirely upon God's mercy and can do nothing else. He leaves the nation's situation with God (although as we shall see in the next section this does not mean that he takes no remedial action). Ezra's response is the response of the humble tax collector in Luke 18:13: 'God have mercy on me, a sinner.' This is all we can say before a holy God.

There can be no doubt that Ezra, on behalf of the nation, is contrite and repentant. We cannot read this prayer and conclude, 'There's no repentance there.' Nevertheless, Ezra does not actually say, 'Please forgive us' or any other similar formula of words, and the fact that he does not helps us see that the true nature of repentance goes much deeper than a few words of apology.

From text to message
Taken together, this prayer and its preamble model how we should think about sin. It has things to teach us about

prayer – and these are a useful by-product – but the main aim is not 'Ezra's school of prayer' so much as 'Ezra's doctrine of sin', which then fuels his prayer.

Getting the message clear: the theme
Ezra responds to the nation's sin by throwing himself on God's mercy.

Getting the message clear: the aim
Grasping the nature of our sin and the character of God is key to approaching Him in Christ Jesus.

A way in
The casual reader will immediately identify the central part that the prayer plays in this section and assume that we are being presented with a model prayer for our own confession. However, our situation is not precisely that of the Israelites and we have no appointed human mediator in quite the way Ezra was (see application below). It is therefore better to help people see that the underlying lessons in this chapter will help us – ultimately – to pray in this kind of way but that Ezra's prayer is not establishing an exact model for us to follow.

Such an approach could begin either positively or negatively. Positively, we could ask people if they longed to pray the way Ezra did or we could encourage them to imagine how much deeper the church's prayer experience would be if these were our kind of prayers. If we desire to pray as Ezra did then we will also need to share Ezra's beliefs.

Negatively, we could ask what someone listening to our prayers might think we believe. It's a sobering exercise and someone eavesdropping on our quiet times (or even our church prayer meeting) might well think we believed in some kind of prosperity gospel or that we thought we were pretty much perfect in the area of godly living.

Ideas for application

- There are strong lines of corporate application here which must not be ignored but which will need careful handling. Sin is not just individual.

- The weight of sin lies heavily upon Ezra because he understood its seriousness. We need to let the text place the same weight upon our own shoulders.

- We also need to recognise what we once were and allow this to magnify the grace that God has shown us in Christ.

- Care needs to be taken to help our hearers grasp that we no longer live under the Old Covenant. Bad things were happening to Israel because of their sin. All our sin is paid for by Christ and therefore any 'bad things' that happen to us are not evidence that we are back under God's judgment. That would be faulty theology. Nevertheless, hard experiences may be evidence of God's fatherly discipline on us as His sons (see Heb. 12).

- Profound prayer of this kind reflects a deep knowledge and experience of God. We cannot manufacture prayer by following liturgy or patterns unless there is this underlying experiential religion.

- In particular, repentance is not just saying 'sorry' to God. It is a deep and heart-felt response to God's character and our own failings which causes us to throw ourselves upon God's mercy.

- There is an unresolved tension here between the justice of God which demands punishment and the mercy of God which does not treat us as our sins deserve. Ultimately these two can only be reconciled at the cross of Christ. We should feel this tension in Ezra's prayer and look towards the place where wrath and mercy meet.

- In one sense, this is a unique Old Covenant prayer. Ezra recognises that the same sins that took the nation into captivity continue to beset the people of God. There is no let up. Simply applying 'must try harder' has not worked – nor has exile, the ultimate Covenant punishment. In this sense, we must appreciate that there is an unresolved tension in the situation Ezra confronts. The people then lived in hope of a better day when hearts would be changed. We can rejoice in that day, for it has now dawned in the giving of the New Covenant in Christ's blood.

Suggestions for preaching

Sermon 1

As I suggested above, Carson's outline (with some adaption) might be a good way to tackle the prayer. We might say humble prayer needs us to understand:

- **What we were:** our sin was terrible and it made our situation desperate.

- **What God has done:** He has graciously restored us, just as He restored the people by bringing them back from captivity.

- **What we are:** but sin still besets us (and very often the same sins)

- **What we now need**: we continue to need God's
  mercy.

This would be an interesting and faithful outline, but as it
stands it fails to include the preamble although this could
be worked in. It also could fall into the trap of equating
the hearts of those then who continued to rebel with
the regenerate hearts that God promises New Covenant
believers.

Sermon 2
An alternative approach could take the chapter as a whole.
In this case, a topical rather than verse by verse approach
might best serve the text. This is particularly the case given
that Ezra's reaction in the opening verses is then reiterated
and confirmed in the words he uses in his prayer.

The true believer/gathered people of God has/have:

- **A realistic grasp of the desperate sinfulness of
  humanity.** Ezra's grief demonstrates that he grasps
  this and in his prayer he is unflinching in laying
  out the sinful events of the past as well as the
  current disobedience.

- **An honest appraisal of the justice of God.** Ezra
  shows such an appraisal in his assessment of the
  people's present captivity (v. 7) and also in his
  realism about the way God's people deserve to be
  treated (v. 14).

- **A majestic experience of the grace of God.** The
  justice of God needs to be seen in the light of
  the grace of God, shown here in the way He has
  brought His people back and preserved a remnant.
  They have not been treated as their sins deserved.

This sermon would need to conclude by establishing that it is in Christ that the justice and mercy of God meet and that it is here that the depravity of humanity is dealt with. However, we need to be honest and say that this approach risks some wrong conclusions being drawn – for example, that when I as a Christian believer sin, I become once again 'unsaved' and therefore in need again (and again and again) of being 're-saved'. A preacher would need to be careful to avoid some of these misconceptions.

Sermon 3

For these reasons it might be best to take an even more applied approach in preaching this passage. In this case the outline would be something like:

- **Only God's grace could save us from the depths of our sin.** This point introduces the tension between God's justice and His mercy *in the context of our original salvation.* This most faithfully reflects the historic aspect of Ezra's petition.

- **Only God's grace can maintain us in fellowship with our holy God.** This second point reflects the current assessment that Ezra gives. He feels the force of ongoing sin and the need to continually rely on the mercy of God and the need to live in continued obedience. The difference for New Covenant believers is that this mercy is historic – it is already given in the finished work of Christ.

All of these approaches need to capture the emotive language that Ezra uses to express his thoughts and to do justice to the fact that his prayer is corporate. It would be too easy for a preacher to neutralise the vocabulary and/ or individualise the applications.

Suggestions for teaching

Questions to help understand the passage

1. What does Ezra learn (v. 1)?

2. What law does this unfaithfulness break (see Deut. 7:3) and why is this disobedience so significant? Think of the history of other kings.

3. What does Ezra's reaction (vv. 3-4) show us?

4. What does Ezra acknowledge about why Israel went into captivity (vv. 6-7)?

5. How have the people experienced God's mercy so far (vv. 8-9)?

6. Why do they continue to need God's mercy (vv. 10-12)?

7. How does Ezra's prayer of confession end (vv. 13-15)? What seems to be missing here compared to what we would usually expect to see in 'a prayer of confession'?

Questions to help apply the passage

1. What do we learn about the depravity of sin from Ezra's words and actions?

2. What do we learn about the mercy of God from reflecting on what He did for Israel?

3. How is the tension between God's justice and mercy ultimately resolved in the Bible?

4. In what sense do we need to continue experiencing the mercy of God?

5. What place does obedience have in the life of a believer?

6. Ezra's prayer is corporate. What does this teach us about our (1) view of sin and (2) praying?

5. Putting things right (Ezra 10:1-44)

Introduction

The text now shifts to the third person again and reports the national steps that were taken to deal with the sin of intermarriage. Words are not enough. They have to be accompanied by actions which prove that the repentance is more than skin-deep. The passage itself is quite straight-forward, the issues it raises considerably less so. Each case of intermarriage is carefully assessed by an appointed com-mission, a process which takes three entire months and is supported by almost the 'whole assembly' (verse 12, in language reminiscent of 3:1).

We are not told the workings of this commission nor presented with any evidence that we can consider. Rather, we are simply given a list of those who were found guilty of this particular sin of Law-breaking. There are one hundred and ten guilty men. This is a small number when viewed as a proportion of all those who had returned. However, the sin is significant enough to warrant the corporate attention it receives.

The challenge of application

It is worth stating at the outset that drawing exact lines of application is tricky. For sure, there is a deliberate ruthlessness in the remedy that we also find for example, in Jesus' words in the Sermon on the Mount, 'If your right hand causes you to stumble, cut it off and throw it away' (Matt. 5:30), though Jesus clearly did not intend His words to be taken literally.

However, beyond this general application of the need to be ruthless in dealing with our sins there will be a variety of views about how we should apply these lessons. Two key questions shape our approach:

First, there is a genuine question about whether the response in chapter 10 is proper or not. As we shall see, commentators take both views with others prevaricating. I believe the tone and context of the text do point in one particular direction as I shall demonstrate below.

Second, even if the response is right we have to think carefully about the interconnection between the Old and New Covenants. That is always a pertinent question but particularly so here. Although all evangelicals see both continuity and discontinuity between the covenants, the measure of each is disputed. A preacher who stresses continuity above discontinuity might draw different lines of application here from a preacher who does the opposite. It is important for preachers to have a strong sense of how the covenants fit together for them to be able to faithfully preach this little section.

Finally, it is worth pointing out that the apparently abrupt ending in our English translations – which can leave us feeling a little hard done by – is less sudden when we remember that the books of Ezra and Nehemiah are actually one book which modern translations have split apart.

Listening to the text

Context and structure
The structure here is very straightforward.

- The remedy proposed (vv. 1-8)
- The inquiry commissioned (vv. 9-15)
- The verdicts delivered (vv. 16-44)

In terms of context, chapter 9 obviously informs much of what is going on here and some of the key themes (e.g. Ezra's grief) are carried over into this section (compare 9:3-4 with verse 6). However, we should also continue to bear in mind Ezra's mission and the overall theme of the book. Ezra is concerned with the Law-keeping of the nation and this itself is a mark of what it means to be in a right relationship with the living God. Lack of obedience and, in particular, marriage to foreign women drove the nation into exile. Therefore, nothing less than the continued existence of the people of God is at stake here (9:13-15). The remedy proposed and implemented in chapter 10 is a 'make or break' one.

Working through the text

The remedy proposed (vv. 1-8)

Ezra's public prayer and demonstration of grief has attracted attention (v. 1) including from those who want to take action. Ezra is not alone (chapter 9 began in the same way). One of those who wants something to be done is named as 'Shekaniah son of Jehiel, one of the descendants of Elam.' We know nothing else about him though it is safe to assume he is some kind of leader or spokesman. He may be one of those Elamites who returned with Ezra (see 8:7) or a descendant of one of the original travellers (2:7). Either way, his proposal is clear.

Like Ezra, Shecaniah recognises the unfaithfulness that the people of God have demonstrated but sees that there is still hope for Israel if something is done. That something is expressed in striking terms, 'Let us make a covenant before our God to send away all these women and their children.'

A covenant here is a solemn promise, rather than a new and additional Bible-Covenant like those God made with Abraham, Moses or David. Alternatively, some commentators suggest that Shecaniah may be proposing that the Israelites 'renew' the Mosaic covenant. However, the language used seems to make this less likely.

Shecaniah makes clear that this suggestion to send away the women and children does not come from him, but is rather, 'in accordance with the counsel of my Lord.' At some point Ezra has already suggested that this is the required remedy and Shecaniah's little speech confirms and supports Ezra in what needs to be done, both legally ('Let it be done according to the Law') and practically ('Rise up; this matter is in your hands. We will support you, so take courage and do it.')

The matter is clearly urgent but it is also difficult. It is no small thing to send people away and therefore Ezra needs to know that people are with him as he embarks on this difficult course of action. He begins by placing the people under oath, an appropriately solemn response, both to the difficult situation and to the making of a 'covenant' promise. Ezra wants to ensure that as they embark on this together, the people will stick with him however painful the process becomes. That the situation is still tense and weighty is confirmed by Ezra's next actions which are to withdraw and mourn, his mourning once again accompanied by fasting.

There is still one further action required, however. So far Ezra's response has been shared by 'a large crowd' (v. 1). He has sought oaths from the 'leading priests and Levites' who have spoken on behalf of 'all Israel' (the probable implication of this phrase in verse 5). But this is still not enough for such a significant moment. So now every single exile is summoned to Jerusalem by proclamation (v. 7). The penalty for non-attendance is twofold: the forfeit of property and exclusion from the worshipping life of the community – both serious consequences.

Why does Ezra need the whole nation to participate? The text is silent but the context provides several answers. One may be entirely practical; it is necessary to gather all those who may be guilty together so that all the cases of intermarriage can be identified. However, given the corporate nature of Ezra's prayer in chapter 9 and the people's response in 10:1-4, it is more likely that Ezra knows that the entire nation must respond appropriately to this call to put things right.

The inquiry commissioned (vv. 9-15)

This gathering takes three days and 'on the twentieth day of the ninth month' (we would say December 458 B.C.) the people of God are all assembled. It is a sober occasion because of what is being addressed, made more so by the incessant rain that is falling (v. 9). Now it is time for Ezra to address the nation.

It is a short speech! In verse 10 Ezra outlines the problem and its consequences. These intermarriages reflect faithlessness to the Lord (compare Mal. 2:10-16). This sin has compounded the nation's guilt (presumably Ezra has in view the entirety of the nation's guilt *up to this point*).

His remedy is simple and has two elements: they must confess their sins to God and they must put right what is wrong ('do his will'). In this particular instance that means separation from other nations and in particular 'from your foreign wives.'

It is worth pointing out at this stage that we are never told more than this in terms of how this putting away actually happened. Were wives simply sent off into the sunset? Were they forcibly removed? Were they returned to their original families? Were they provided for in any way and if so, how?

What happened to their children (who get a brief mention in v. 44)?

The straight answer to all these questions is the same: we simply do not know. Any application which is therefore based on imagined answers to these enigmas is pure speculation and we would do well to avoid that. Some listeners might have serious objections to the severity of what was proposed and such concerns might be allayed by suggesting that, for example, the actions might have been more compassionate than imagined; however, such responses are still speculative.

What *is* clear is that the entire nation responds positively to the plan to remedy the situation. 'You are right! We must do as you say.' There are however two practical objections. One is the sheer scale of the task. It will take a while to work through all the families of the nation. 'There are many people here' and there are many cases ('we have sinned greatly in this thing' v. 13). The second is that even if it were possible to work through the great number of families, it is still raining (in fact it is the 'rainy season') and thus it is impractical for everyone to stand around whilst the investigation is carried out.

So a proposal is made to set up what we might today call an inquiry. We need to be careful using this language because to our modern ears it sounds like the sort of thing that gets set up to mediate between competing views. There is no mediation here. The nation speaks as one. The commission is established for purely practical reasons. It will be presided over by 'elders and judges', language which implies some investigation will be necessary.[19]

---

19. For example, a foreign wife who had converted to Judaism was presumably exempt from the putting away, as the Law allowed such practice.

Interestingly there are, amongst the whole nation, four objectors: two key men supported by two others (v. 15). Somewhat enigmatically, we are not told what they objected *to*? Did they not like the principle? Or were they objecting to the proposal? Did they want it to go faster? Slower, perhaps? At the end of the day all we can say is that these names are recorded for us – almost certainly to show how well accepted the proposals were, for if only four names can be found out of a nation of tens of thousands (and probably more by now) we can see how universally acceptable this remedy was.[20]

Was this the right remedy?

That brings us to a key question: was this the right way to fix the problem? To our modern ears it sounds like a very harsh approach. Carson outlines two views, suggesting that on the one hand, the situation is 'something akin to a revival...one must deal radically with sin.'[21] On the other hand, 'the steps that flow from it are virtually all wrong. Marriage, after all, is a creation ordinance.' Furthermore, he states, 'Strictly speaking the text does not adjudicate between these two interpretations, though the first of the two is slightly more natural within the stance of the book.' He then concludes by saying, 'I suspect that in large measure both views are correct. There is something noble and courageous about the action taken; there is also something heartless and reductionistic.'

---

20. There are places in Scripture, of course, where an overwhelming majority view is incorrect: think of Joshua and Caleb and the nation in Numbers 13-14 or, indeed, the baying crowds demanding the release of Barabbas (e.g. Matt. 27). But the overwhelming sense in Ezra is that when the nation is united, it is for good.

21. Carson, D. A., *For the love of God, volume 2*, entry for 10 January.

With the greatest respect to Dr Carson, I believe he prevaricates too much. True, the text is silent on whether this is the proper approach. But the clear implication of this whole section beginning at chapter 7 is that Ezra is God's man come to do God's job. He is learned in the Law and now we discover that he has the backing of 99.9% of the nation. This remedy is not 'heartless and reductionistic' but necessary and 'done according to the Law' (v. 3).

Perhaps the situation becomes clearer if we reflect on the nature of the marriages. Carson argues that marriage is a creation ordinance. But we have to ask, were these actual marriages? I would argue that marriage and divorce are the wrong categories to apply. 'Foreign women were married contrary to the law of God. The marriages were illegal from the outset.'[22]

This, I believe, is a very helpful way of assessing the situation. To use a modern parallel, it would be like a man who is married but who then runs off and marries a second woman, something totally contrary to the law. Or, to be more blunt, this is akin to someone marrying a relative to whom marriage is prohibited. There is no question of divorce in these cases; the marriage is not actually a marriage from the outset, for it breaks the law. In both cases, the law does not allow the situation to continue, whatever the feelings or needs of the two individuals.

Of course, these are modern civil illustrations where marriage is governed by the state; Israel, however, was a theocracy under the Law of Moses. Nevertheless, such illustrations serve a useful purpose as they demonstrate the way we should think of these marriages in Ezra: that

---

22. Fensham, p. 135.

is, as being illegitimate in the first place. Such an approach answers the technical questions but still gives rise to questions about appropriate contemporary applications and these will be considered below.

The verdicts delivered (vv. 16-44)

We return to the text. Ezra appoints a representative panel ('one from each family division' v. 16) and the commission begins, starting on the first day of the tenth month and completing its work by the first day of the first month (March 457 B.C.). The whole process takes seventy-five days.

Verse 18 onwards is the third of the lists in the book of Ezra and whilst the first two represent those whose hearts God moved to return, this last one serves a different purpose. It is a shameful list of those found guilty of marrying foreign women. There are one hundred and ten cases in all from all groups within the nation:

- Priests, including the family of the previous High Priest, Joshua, vv. 18-22

- Levites, v. 23

- Singers and Gatekeepers v. 24

- Other Israelites, vv. 25-43

These groups appear in reverse order to their order in chapter 2 (probably making a point about the very different nature of this list). All parts of the nation are affected by this disobedience and each guilty party is identified by name. There is some speculation that the commission moved very slowly (one hundred and ten cases over seventy-five days which, allowing for Sabbaths and Festivals, still accounts for less than two cases per day). However, whilst that may be the case, we have no idea how many other cases were considered but were subsequently found not to have broken the requirements of the Mosaic Law.

Verse 44 ends abruptly. 'All these had married foreign women, and some of them had children by these wives.' Although not mentioned at this point, verse 3 implies that the children were sent away with their mothers. This abrupt ending is explained by the connection to Nehemiah (see note above) but also serves the purpose of leaving readers feeling unsatisfied. This itself is useful and Fyall is worth quoting at length:

'Ezra [is a] light shining in the darkness until the morning star arises. In the bigger story, Ezra is pointing to a holy city where holy people will live and God's presence will be with them continually. This remnant is the proof that God had not finished with his people and that "the nations will know that I, the Lord, make Israel holy" (Ezek. 37:28). It lays the groundwork for the appearing of Jesus Christ and so Ezra, like many other Biblical books, ends on an unfinished note, but God's purposes continue and will one day come to fulfilment.'[23]

From text to message
As noted throughout, the preacher needs to steer a very careful course because though this is a straightforward passage in terms of its *meaning*, it is a complex one in terms of its *application*. The one, of course, informs the other. As with other similar passages, preachers should ensure the entire passage is read out: even the list of miscreants is inspired Scripture.

Getting the message clear: the theme
The nation universally decides to deal comprehensively with the sin that has crept in.

---

23. Fyall, p. 137.

Getting the message clear: the aim

In broadest terms, this is about the ruthlessness with which Christians must fight sin. We need to take care to avoid false applications (e.g. Christians, divorce your unbelieving spouses). For that reason, applications must be checked carefully against the New Testament commands, particularly those found in the Epistles.

A way in

The issue at stake is what you do with a serious problem. A medical analogy might work – for example, the difference between treating symptoms and causes. If deadly sin is to be rooted out then the remedy must be radical. Alternatively, the preacher can head off the objections from the outset. It would not be inappropriate to empathise with hearers (for example, after the reading and at the beginning of the sermon) by asking the question they are all imagining anyway! 'What is that all about? Sounds pretty grim!' The preacher can then say, 'I'm going to show you why this is not what you may first think it is, and how it is a message about sin that every believer needs to hear and embrace.'

Ideas for application

- In broad terms the message is clear: we must view sin soberly and deal with it ruthlessly. This is the same point picked up by Jesus in the Sermon on the Mount (Matt. 5:29-30); it is also present in the Epistles (for example, Eph. 5:3). We are often far too accommodating of sin; we fail to see the seriousness of it and fail to exercise any effort in putting it away. Our battle against sin is real and necessary.

- More particularly, it is important to say what the application *is not*. This is not about divorcing unbelieving spouses. The New Testament is categorical in saying that divorce in these situations is neither desirable nor required. 1 Corinthians 7 is particularly pertinent and whilst it is addressing a particular situation (when one spouse has been converted post marriage), it is clear that the spiritual mismatch does not invalidate the marriage itself.

- Nevertheless, there is a more general point to be made about the effect that being 'yoked to unbelievers' (2 Cor. 6:14) does have. Paul's application here is almost certainly not about marriage; he is making a broader point which stands out from our Ezra passage too. If churches allow themselves to be influenced by those who do not profess Christ then the results will be ultimately catastrophic. Arguably, this is the story of many Christian denominations and remarkably, there are even evangelical churches who allow unbelievers on to committees and into leaderships (of various kinds).

- We see in Ezra 10 that this sin is corporate both in its effect and its remedy. The sins of individuals affect the whole nation and must be addressed corporately. We fail to weep over the corporate effect that sin has upon us as a community and relegate its remedy to the action of individuals rather than thinking about how we can fight ungodliness together.

- Readers must also continue to see the big picture of the book – God is sovereignly working so that His people can worship *and* obey Him. Worship which is not matched by a desire to please the Lord (e.g. 2 Cor. 5:9) is empty and meaningless.

- Finally, there is an unresolved tension which is only addressed by the coming of Christ. The sins that need to be tackled here are the same old sins which brought the nation down and we must feel some of this burden – 'not this again!' – which only the coming of the Saviour and the New Covenant will relieve.

Suggestions for preaching

Sermon 1

One sermon could follow the narrative structure of the material, broadly using the outline given above, that is:

- **The remedy proposed** (vv. 1-8)

- **The inquiry commissioned** (vv. 9-15)

- **The verdicts delivered** (vv. 16-44)

My personal view is that whilst such a sermon would be adequate, it would be little more. Whilst this approach could be improved by using more gripping headings, e.g. **a radical solution to a deep problem** (vv. 1-8), the narrative of the passage is clear and the story does not need to be retold. There are complex application issues at stake here and the earlier they can be introduced the better.

Sermon 2

An alternative approach is to drive home applications from the outset, for example:

- **Deadly sin has to be radically expelled.**
  This point picks up on the seriousness of sin,
  something which has already been seen in chapter
  9 and is carried through to chapter 10 (e.g. v. 6).
  It also gives due attention to the comprehensive
  manner in which sin is dealt with. The preacher
  will have to deal with any expected objections at
  this point.

- **Individual sin has to be corporately recognised.**
  It is hard to ignore the corporate nature of this
  remedy; we see it in the way the chapter begins
  and the manner in which the whole nation is
  invited to take part. The list at the end, recorded
  for posterity, reinforces this point.

- **Joyful obedience is the mark of true worshippers.**
  The entire book reaches its climax with a focus
  on obedience not simply as a grudging law-
  keeping but the joyful delight of people who have
  been brought into a right relationship with God.
  This is the place to identify the unresolved issue
  which nags away all through the whole of the Old
  Testament; unless something radical changes, the
  nation will keep on self-destructing.

Such headings might not correspond to exact verse and
paragraph divisions but will give the sense of what the
passage is trying to convey more clearly. This last point
brings the book to a close.

Suggestions for teaching
This will be a study where strong leadership is required to
make sure the discussion is not derailed.

Questions to help understand the passage

1. Remind yourselves of why Ezra is weeping and mourning (v. 1 and v. 6) and why he is joined by other Israelites (v. 1). You may have to look back into chapter 9 for answers.

2. What is shocking about Shecaniah's suggestion in verses 2-4? How do we know it is the right thing to do?

3. Why do you suppose an oath is needed (v. 5)?

4. Why do the rest of the nation need to be summoned (v. 7)?

5. Why can the inquiry not respond immediately (v. 13)?

6. How long does the inquiry take?

7. Why are the names of those found guilty preserved in Scripture, do you suppose?

Questions to help apply the passage

1. How does this help us, *in general terms*, think about the seriousness of sin and what must be done to tackle it, both as individuals and as a church?

2. How does your church deal with sin when it arises?

3. What seems to be the obvious application? Why do we know this is not right? (The leader will need to read the notes above carefully to lead a group through this question.)

4. What do we learn about the dangers of allowing non-Christian influences into the church?

5. How has the book of Ezra shown us the connection between true worship and joyful obedience? Why are both necessary?

6. How does this passage leave us longing for the coming of Christ? What difference does the promise of His coming make to us, especially in the battle against sin?

FURTHER READING

Of the many books on Ezra (often coupled together with commentaries on Nehemiah), these are among the most useful.

Breneman, Martin, *Ezra, Nehemiah & Esther* (Nashville, USA: Broadman & Holman, 1993).

Fensham, Charles, NICOT: *Ezra & Nehemiah* (Grand Rapids, USA: Eerdmans, 1996). I have found this the most useful 'technical' (i.e. verse by verse) commentary.

Fyall, Robert, *The message of Ezra and Haggai* (Nottingham, UK: IVP, 2010).

Hamilton, James, *Christ-centred exposition, Ezra and Nehemiah* (Nashville, USA: Holman Reference, 2014).

Holmgren, Frederick, *Ezra & Nehemiah* (Grand Rapids, USA: Eerdmans, 1987).

Kidner, Derek, *Ezra & Nehemiah* (Nottingham, UK: IVP, 1979).

McConville, J. G., *Ezra, Nehemiah & Esther* (Louisville, USA: Westminster John Knox: 1985).

Throntvelt, Mark, *Ezra-Nehemiah* (Louisville, USA: Westminster John Knox: 1992).

Williams, Peter, *Opening up Ezra* (Leominster, UK: Day One Publications, 2006).

Williamson, H. G. M., *Ezra, Nehemiah* (Dallas, USA: Word, 1998).

APPENDIX I:
THE CYRUS CYLINDER

The Cyrus Cylinder has been described as one of the most important finds in biblical archaeology and it is helpful for the preacher of Ezra to know a little more about it and its background. King Cyrus (more precisely, Cyrus the Great or Cyrus II) founded the Persian empire (conquering Babylon) and he ruled from 538/9 B.C. until his death in 530 B.C. But he had been a great conqueror up to that key Bible moment, conquering lands we would now recognise as Iran and Turkey. He is not only a key figure in antiquity, Cyrus is also explicitly mentioned in Isaiah's prophecies as the one who will deliver Israel from Babylonian bondage (see Isa. 44:28, 45:1 and 45:13). However, to make sense of the edict of Ezra chapter 1 (and the cylinder), we need to go a bit further back in history.

The settlement policies of conquerors loom large in the book of Ezra. After their conquest of the northern tribes, the Assyrians resettled Samaria with peoples from every other conquered land (see 2 Kings 17:24-41). The end result there was a kind of syncretistic religion which included elements of Yahweh worship mixed with the idolatry of other nations (see 2 Kings 17:41). This is the worship of the enemies of Judah which Zerubbabel and Joshua see through in Ezra 4. It is also almost certainly the background behind the Samaritan-Jewish divide that dominates so many of the gospel stories. Babylonian aggression however took a different form; their policy after conquests was to exile entire peoples to their own capital city and its environs (2 Kings 25:11), thus Jerusalem was left in ruins.

Ezra 1 suggests that Persian Cyrus reversed this Babylonian policy, allowing exiles to return and rebuild their places of worship. Of course, the focus in Ezra is on Jewish exiles with no mention made of the other nations which Babylon conquered. Up until relatively recently there was no historical evidence which corroborated this shift of policy: indeed, to many critical historians it seemed a highly unlikely decision. Cultic worship was at the centre of life and national identity for many nations (not just Israel) and therefore a decision to allow exiles to return *and* rebuild their places of worship seemed improbable, at best.

Then in 1879 the archaeologist Hormuzd Rassan discovered a clay cylinder (in two parts) which had been dug into the foundation of a temple in Babylon itself. The cylinder is covered in writing using an ancient script called cuneiform and is about 22cm long and 10cm in diameter. The trip, sponsored by the British Museum, had acquired permission from the ruling Sultan to bring any finds back to the UK. The cylinder is now one of the British Museum's most precious exhibits.

The cylinder itself is a typical document of the time. It is not the precise edict of Ezra 1; but it does confirm the veracity of the Bible text. The cylinder gives details of a more general edict which allowed all peoples to return to their homelands: the chapter 1 edict would have been a  subset of this one. The cylinder has been called 'the first human rights charter' and a copy of it is displayed in the foyer of the United Nations building in New York. However, more recent critical analysis has tended to focus on the 'marketing' nature of the edict – whether, in other words, this was simply a way of Cyrus showing himself to be the beneficent king he longed to be known as. Whether or not this critique is fair, the Bible point remains unchallenged: Cyrus, against all the policies of his predecessors, did allow the Jews to return to Jerusalem and rebuild the Temple unchallenged. This, in part at least, is the reason the work got finished (see Ezra 6:14).

The consequence of the 1879 find is that the historicity of Ezra 1 is no longer up for debate. Historians still argue over the reason that Cyrus made such an about turn but, as evangelicals, we know that Ezra 1 provides the answer to this conundrum too even though some would not like the answer. For here is the evidence that God moved the heart of the king.

There is more information about the cylinder on the British Museum website and the artefact is well worth viewing for those within reach of London although it should be noted that it is sometimes loaned out to other institutions. I have included a selection of quotations from it in translation below to give a flavour of the text itself. The picture above is not of the cylinder itself (which is hard to photograph behind the reflective glass) but of the author's

own copy held in my hand to give some idea of size. The
Museum also contains many other treasures from this
period which, although not directly related to Bible stories,
nevertheless give visitors a feel for its times and places,
particularly for the court life with which Daniel, Esther,
Ezra and Nehemiah would have been very familiar.[1]

> I am Cyrus, king of the universe, the great king, the powerful
> king, king of Babylon, king of Sumer and Akkad, king of the
> four quarters of the world, son of Cambyses, the great king,
> king of the city of Anshan....When I went as harbinger of
> peace i[nt]o Babylon I founded my sovereign residence within
> the palace amid celebration and rejoicing. Marduk, the great
> lord, bestowed on me as my destiny the great magnanimity
> of one who loves Babylon, and I every day sought him out
> in awe..... As for the population of Babylon [..., w]ho as if
> without div[ine intention] had endured a yoke not decreed
> for them, I soothed their weariness; I freed them from their
> bonds. Marduk, the great lord, rejoiced at [my good] deeds,
> and he pronounced a sweet blessing over me, Cyrus, the king
> who fears him...From [Shuanna] I sent back to their places
> to the city of Ashur and Susa, Akkad, the land of Eshnunna,
> the city of Zamban, the city of Meturnu, Der, as far as the
> border of the land of Guti – the sanctuaries across the river
> Tigris – whose shrines had earlier become dilapidated, the
> gods who lived therein, and made permanent sanctuaries for
> them. I collected together all of their people and returned
> them to their settlements, and the gods of the land of Sumer
> and Akkad which Nabonidus – to the fury of the lord of
> the gods – had brought into Shuanna, at the command of
> Marduk, the great lord, I returned them unharmed to their

---

1. An indispensable guide is the superb Edwards, B. & Anderson, C.,
Through the British Museum with the Bible, Fourth Edition (Leominster,
UK: Day One Publications, 2013). There is really nothing else quite like it.

cells, in the sanctuaries that make them happy. May all the gods that I returned to their sanctuaries, every day before Bel and Nabu, ask for a long life for me, and mention my good deeds...[2]

---

2. See British Museum website, www.britishmuseum.org. The words in brackets are unclear on the cylinder and have been added in, using other contemporary documents as a base.

Appendix 2:

Comparing Ezra 2 and Nehemiah 7

The long list of names in Ezra 2 is repeated in Nehemiah 7, the companion Bible book. However, the careful reader will notice some differences. In broad terms:

- The list of names given in Ezra 2:2 contains only eleven names whereas the equivalent list in Nehemiah 7 has twelve names. Also, two of the names in the Ezra list are significantly different from those in Nehemiah and others have variant spellings.

- The list of names given in Ezra 2:3-35 is almost entirely the same in both books with one exception (Magbish in Ezra 2:30, who does not appear in Neh. 7).

- The numbers of each tribe contain more differences, particularly those in Ezra 2:6-20.

- Other differences are relatively minor (for example, the 652 in Ezra 2:60 is 642 in Neh. 7:62).

What are evangelicals with a high view of Scripture to make of these differences? Our belief in Scripture is in the Scriptures as originally given. Hebrew is a highly complex script with very slight variations in accent making large differences in words. Moreover, numbers are notoriously difficult to present – there are no digits; all numbers have to be written out fully.

No doubt this might account for some of the differences. Such differences should not undermine our doctrine of Scripture, properly understood. However, there is also a clue in the text that these records may come from different sources. We are not told explicitly where the Ezra record comes from but it seems to be an integral part of the story of the exiles' return. However, the Nehemiah account is introduced in a different way: Nehemiah convenes the people of God in Jerusalem almost ninety years later and finds there a list. 'I found the genealogical record of those who had been the first to return. This is what I found written there' (Neh. 7:5). In other words, Nehemiah does not represent his list as an accurate rendition of Ezra 2. Rather, he represents it as an accurate representation of what he discovered in Jerusalem. It may be a copy of a copy of the original, for example. As such, minor differences neither undermine this particular text (Ezra 2) nor our doctrine of Scripture. Crucially, the lessons that flow from Ezra 2 are not – for the main part – dependent on harmonising the lists.

More detail about the differences can be found in a technical commentary.

Also available in the *Teaching* Series...

TEACHING
ISAIAH

Unlocking Isaiah for
the Bible Teacher

DAVID JACKMAN

SERIES EDITORS: DAVID JACKMAN & ROBIN SYDSERFF

978-1-8455-0565-3

Teaching Isaiah

Unlocking Isaiah for the Bible Teaching

DAVID JACKMAN

In the period that Isaiah the prophet lived there was immense political upheaval across the ancient near-east. The people of God had a choice – to follow their own human policies or to follow the promises of God. They chose to be unfaithful. The prophet breaks in and calls them to repent asking them to stop violating the covenant. In today's setting this is a message that your hearers will identify with, readily identifying ourselves with the deceitful hearts of the people of Judah, and learn also from their mistakes how our own divided hearts may equally lead us astray. This is not another commentary but a useful resource, which will help the pastor/ preacher, a small group leader or a youth worker communicate a message of grace when speaking from the book of Isaiah. It will give you help in planning and executing a lesson in particular with background, structure, key points and application.

PT RESOURCES

TEACHING
AMOS

From text to message

BOB FYALL

SERIES EDITORS: DAVID JACKMAN & ROBIN SYDSERFF

978-1-8455-0142-6

Teaching Amos

From text to message

Bob Fyall

'Teaching Amos' is written by Dr Bob Fyall, who has a particular passion for preaching and teaching the Old Testament. He is author of a number of books, including the Focus on the Bible volume on Daniel.

Having first outlined a number of possible approaches to constructing a series of sermons or talks on Amos, Bob unlocks the text based on a suggested structure of nine sermons or talks. Individual chapters are specifically geared towards working from text to sermon, combining rigorous exposition with relevant application, always with an eye to the main teaching point of the passage.

This volume will not only encourage better preaching on Amos, but serve as a timely reminder of the striking relevance of the prophet's message for today.

TEACHING
PSALMS

Volume1: From text to message

CHRISTOPHER ASH

SERIES EDITORS: DAVID JACKMAN & ADRIAN REYNOLDS

978-1-5271-0004-6

Teaching Psalms Vol.1

From Text to Message

Christopher Ash

The Psalms can be sung, spoken or read – but they were written to be prayed. Until we pray them from the heart we miss their purpose. If you love, or want to love, or think perhaps you ought to love, the Psalms, this first instalment of a two-volume set on the Psalter is for you. Christopher Ash gives us a practical and theological handbook to equip us to pray and to teach the Psalms. He faces the difficulties and shows how praying them in Christ does justice to their original meaning and context as well as their place in the whole bible.

Christian Focus Publications

Our mission statement –

STAYING FAITHFUL
In dependence upon God we seek to impact the world through literature faithful to His infallible Word, the Bible. Our aim is to ensure that the Lord Jesus Christ is presented as the only hope to obtain forgiveness of sin, live a useful life and look forward to heaven with Him.

Our books are published in four imprints:

CHRISTIAN
FOCUS

Popular works including biographies, commentaries, basic doc-trine and Christian living.

CHRISTIAN
HERITAGE

Books representing some of the best material from the rich heritage of the church.

MENTOR

Books written at a level suitable for Bible College and seminary students, pastors, and other serious readers. The imprint includes commentaries, doctrinal studies, examination of current issues and church history.

CF4•K

Children's books for quality Bible teaching and for all age groups: Sunday school curriculum, puzzle and activity books; personal and family devotional titles, biographies and inspirational stories – because you are never too young to know Jesus!

Christian Focus Publications Ltd,
Geanies House, Fearn, Ross-shire,
IV20 1TW, Scotland, United Kingdom.
www.christianfocus.com